Style and substance

LEADERSHIP AND THE COLLEGE PRESIDENCY

Louis T. Benezet
Joseph Katz
Frances W. Magnusson

AMERICAN COUNCIL ON EDUCATION
Washington, D. C.

© 1981 American Council on Education
One Dupont Circle, Washington, D.C. 20036

Library of Congress Cataloging in Publication Data

Benezet, Louis Tomlinson, 1915–
    Style and substance.

    Bibliography: p.
    1. College presidents—United States.   2. Leadership.
I. Katz, Joseph, 1920–   II. Magnusson, Frances W.
III. American Council on Education.   IV. Title.
LB2341.B439   378'.111   81-17679
ISBN 0-8268-1456-5   AACR2

9   8   7   6   5   4   3   2   1

Printed in the United States of America

Contents

Preface

This book traces its origin to research interests of my colleague Joseph Katz in 1969. In that work he was associated with Carol Leland and Lewis Mayhew. Some time after joining the faculty at Stony Brook in 1975, I had the congenial idea of joining to Katz's interests my own ideas that had emerged from a succession of presidential tours at four institutions. To understand the office of presidency in its present setting and in light of current events in U.S. higher education, we decided to launch the Presidency Project.

The Presidency Project obtained its data between 1976 and 1979 from interviews with the presidents, senior academic administrators, faculty, and students at twenty-five colleges and universities. Enrollment at these institutions ranged from just over 1,000 to 55,000. The institutions are located throughout the country, from the Southwest and the deep South to the Midwest and Middle Atlantic states to northern New England. Eight are private coeducational liberal arts colleges; three are private women's colleges. Seven are state universities: one is in the Ivy League; another is perennially among the top recipients of federal research grants. Two are large public colleges, each a part of a university system.

The essence of the book is the statements of the nearly 250 persons who were interviewed. One highlight of the Presidency Project's findings was the near-unanimity expressed as to the need for college presidents to carry out the full measure of their office. Virtually everyone interviewed believed that their college or university should be effectively managed and sensitively led by men and women who are equal to the full personal dimensions of the task. To be sure, each president's approach to fulfilling that obligation incurred ample criticism on that campus.

Appropriately, our inquiries concentrated on the discussions with the presidents. This book, which has evolved from the Presidency Project, contains material from other sources, but the presidential interviews, along with the recorded views of key faculty persons, provide the basis for most of the conclusions. In nearly all cases, before interviewing the presidents, we asked them to write an essay about recent experiences they felt could be considered personal leadership of the institution's course of events. The essays, which were mailed to us before the interviews, became useful take-off points for discussion in the interviews.

The aim of the interviews was to explore the human dynamics of the college presidency. The resulting book examines the place of individual leadership in institutions of higher education in the 1980s. Thus, the interview with the president stressed his or her review of prospects for providing growth (in the broadest cognitive sense) for students, professors, and professional specialists—in short, for each person associated with the venture.

To discover what people around the president thought about his or her views of institutional direction, the survey team spoke with persons sufficiently familiar with the executive office to discuss the current administration (anonymity was assured). Interviews were held with other senior administrators, particularly the chief academic officer; with faculty members active in key groups such as the faculty senate; and with upperclassmen connected with some aspect of campus governance, such as the education policy committee or a president advisership in a dormitory.

Transcripts representing over 250 hours of conversation at these twenty-five institutions thus provided the data for this study. The comments were candid, often colorful, and occasionally dramatic. The combined report presents three analyses, based on the same transcribed interviews, of the leadership of the American college president as viewed both by those who are charged with providing it and by those who are directly affected by it. The analyses give viewpoints that one of our group has compared to the Japanese drama *Rashomon*, in which different characters recreate their own versions of the same incident.

The 250 conversations corroborate developments that contemporary writers in higher education see already in motion (see, for example, *The Modern American College*, by Arthur Chickering and associates). These trends include the following:

- College clientele will continue to broaden with respect to age, sex, financial status, ethnic and international background, prior experience, patterns of attendance, and individual purposes for learning.
- Likewise, the professoriat will continue to broaden with respect to teaching fields, average age (faculty members will be older), part-

time interests and occupations, and extent of professional involvement in nonteaching aspects of their institutions.

- Student interest in governance sharing will vary according to school tradition and forms of control, yet the general trend will be toward greater involvement.
- The effective president of the future will be less a potentate of a small separate kingdom and more a catalyst of dynamic contacts involving faculty members, students, and a variety of educational environments. The home campus will serve mainly as a base for learning experiences in many places.

Chapter 1, an overview of other writers' observations of presidential leadership, provides a context for our own study. In Chapter 2, Joseph Katz presents various dilemmas that arise when presidents use the powers of their office while remaining aware (some less than others) of traditions of faculty power. Faculty members dislike both the devious use of executive power and the nice-guy syndrome, in which a president professes to make major campus decisions in a democratic fashion.

In Chapter 3, Frances Magnusson traces fact and opinion about the gap that separates the chief executive from the academic community. Chapter 4 examines how these presidents execute the responsibilities of their office—how they see their actions and how they see the impact of these actions on others. This chapter covers a range of options that the presidents interviewed took to resolve the conundrums unique to leadership in higher education.

While preparing this study, the survey team enjoyed at every campus a cordial welcome and a spirit of cooperation—indeed, an active interest in seeing the record fully written. For this response we are most grateful. We are especially indebted to Dr. Carol Leland, who conducted several of the campus visits, including some that were farthest away from the project center.

The Presidency Project campus visits were made possible in large part by grants from the Lilly Endowment and from the Exxon Education Foundation. We are particularly grateful to the twenty-five college and university presidents, each of whom went beyond ordinary collegiality to display a sincere and vital interest in helping the Presidency Project become a valid statement of presidential beliefs and actions. Without that uniform expression of active interest, the study could not have been made and this book could not have been written.

Louis T. Benezet

1 Perceptions of the Presidency

The American college and university presidency has been the subject of at least a dozen books and hundreds of articles during the past twenty years. The issues confronting the leader of a community dedicated to the intellect seem naturally to arouse curiosity. Recent preoccupation with national leadership (or its absence) has prompted the comparison with leadership in higher education. In fact, two presidents of the United States—Woodrow Wilson and Dwight Eisenhower—have also served as university presidents.

Twelve million people are currently enrolled in college or university courses for formal credit toward a degree. As a result, the public has become increasingly aware of the position of college and university presidents and their considerable power. How an executive can direct a community of scholars, many of whom may be more intellectually gifted than he or she, is puzzling to many people. Yet for decades now, the president of an institution has not necessarily been its leading scholar.

What powers does a college or university president have? Current writings on the position stress the president's labors over budget stretching, retrenched programs, and the prospect of serious enrollment shortages through the mid-1990s. As competition increases for resources already attenuated by inflation and enrollment loss, the job of presiding over an institution becomes increasingly a job of learning techniques for motivating the faculty, staff, and students.

The president's responsibility to be an education leader is presumably his or her primary responsibility, although literature about this role is not easy to find. John Maguire asserts: "At a minimum the college president concerned to be an educational leader will exhibit a certain stance toward learning and the work of the intellect."[1] One

1. John D. Maguire, "The President as Educational Leader," *The President as Educational Leader* (Washington, D.C.: Association of American Colleges, 1976), p. 10.

would think that presidential search committees and boards would routinely include leadership qualities in their criteria, but they do not necessarily do so.

Recent publications have underscored realistic expectations of the office. They take account of enrollment declines and other fiscal constraints; the narrowing access to the centers of education policy making; the enlarged role of negotiation as a means of implementing change; the impact of the president's style on the institution; and the president's function in setting institutional goals. Some of this literature is optimistic, some merely descriptive, some ironic or disparaging. Some is written from the viewpoint of organization theory and treats the position of president mainly as a single entity in a large organization. Books written during the past twenty years underscore a continuing trend: the office of president is seen as declining in educational significance while becoming more and more managerial.

Such findings pose certain dilemmas for persons both on and off campus who are trying to find the center of an institution's education policy making. The question keeps recurring: Can the president lead as an educator, or is he or she merely an executive director managing one of many complex social organizations?

Harold Stoke, in *The American College President* (1959), defines the president's major function as clarifying the institution's purposes and selecting the appropriate means to achieve them. Stoke sees the president's influence on education declining because of specialization that forces presidents to be managers and faculty members to be scholars. The president's administrative duties are more "insistent" than his intellectual interests, and it is impossible for the president to keep up with current scholarship.

Harold Dodds also deplores the amount of a president's time taken up by details outside the realm of teaching, learning, and discovery. In *The Academic President: Educator or Caretaker?* (1962), Dodds states his belief that a president can exercise choice in the matter and influence the faculty members, who must also decide how much time to devote to institutional policy and how much to devote to their own scholarship.

Dodds's thesis is based on a curious denigration of the college presidency. The American professoriate's concern with the educative process is so intense that presidents have been known to give up their posts and return to teaching to regain "respectability" with their colleagues. The problem may stem from the fact that the American professoriate—unlike the British professoriate, for example—does not highly esteem the systematic study of education. If a president of an Ivy League university were to confront that problem head on, he or she might help the academic community tolerate what the administration must do to keep the university machinery in gear.

Too many books by presidents are written in the years immediately following campus controversies in which they were participants—controversies that often resulted in their departure from office. Because personal perspective is rarely objective, the resulting volumes seldom increase knowledge about the position of president. Thus, persons interested in the college presidency should be aware that many of these authors left the presidency under unfortunate circumstances and at a time not entirely of their own choosing. In this category belongs a large number of books, beginning with Dexter M. Keezer's *The Light That Flickers* (1947) and including Warren G. Bennis's *The Leaning Ivory Tower* (1973) and Gail T. Parker's *The Writing on the Wall: Inside Higher Education in America* (1979). These books reflect almost continuous battles between the president and administrators or between the president and professors, other administrators, college patrons, or interested citizens; at times, college administration seems to be nothing but strife. Of course, some embattled presidents have left their positions because they were on the just side of a losing cause. The net effect of these books, however, is to publicize the college presidency as a futile exercise with little more status than a cat-and-dog fight confers on the beclawed referee.

Michael D. Cohen and James G. March, in *Leadership and Ambiguity: The American College President* (1974), state that the college or university president has more potential to influence the institution than any other person in the institution but is perceived as having *less* power. They see the president as not knowing exactly what he or she can do or should be doing to affect policy. They maintain that the president is probably mistaken to imagine he or she can have a significant long-term effect on the institution's position. Because of the nature of the institution, which Cohen and March characterize as "organized anarchy," they conclude that the president's major responsibility is "to lead the organization to a changing and more complex view of itself by treating goals as only partly knowable."[2]

An additional note on *Leadership and Ambiguity* is needed because of the impact of its catch phrases describing the college presidency. "Organized anarchy" is but one of many deflating phrases

2. Michael D. Cohen and James G. March, *Leadership and Ambiguity: The American College President* (New York: McGraw-Hill, 1974), p. 206.

the authors use to describe what they call a mythology of goals, purposes, policies, and rational planning in guiding centers of higher learning. References to deliberately overloading the system, the "garbage-can tactic," and the "technology of foolishness" reflect a certain archness, which is interspersed with hard data and analyses of political realities in academe. The effect of the book has perhaps been to help arm the professoriate against a president's zealousness and, at the same time, to lessen administrators' guilt about not taking hold of the academic machinery as they should.

Students of institutional leadership must learn to separate the solid contributions of this literature from whimsical conclusions. Some statements about the presidency—for example, that the president's contribution may be measured by his or her capability for sustaining a creative interaction of foolishness and rationality— simply are not helpful. By comparison, James MacGregor Burns's general treatise *Leadership* (1978) is meat for discussion.

Leadership and Ambiguity has been a popular book among presidents. Its popularity can be explained in part because the authors have reassured executives that a "transforming leadership"—Burns's concept—can be neither expected nor controlled. If a leadership that changes people and circumstances can neither be expected nor controlled, then there is no use in attempting to provide such leadership, and the executive's conscience need not be vexed any longer.

Reflected in *Leadership and Ambiguity* is the authors' evident reluctance to decide how to connect their findings with their phrasings. The latter float free of the data on public images of presidents, measures of stress and authoritarianism, how executives fit their colleges, extrapolations of a president's tenure, and so on. In contrast, their analyses of leadership rely less on data than on personal accounts of presidents' sweating against resistive academic departments. The insights are entertaining if the reader seeks a caricature of organization in academe. But are they also accurate and predominantly true? Do they offer anything on which to build?

For centuries, Cambridge and Oxford endured marvels of impromptu organization (or nonorganization) founded on layers of scholarly and ecclesiastical tradition. (Who would wish to describe the workings of the hebdomadal council, for example?) Out of Oxford and Cambridge came most of England's leaders for seven hundred years. Perhaps the answer points to one-on-one teaching by the dons; perhaps it hints of subtleties among the heads of colleges that thus far have resisted charting; perhaps it is a flat assertion that a country's best leaders will come from its most intelligent citizens (for most of those centuries, of course, Oxford and Cambridge's admissions process reflected social class rather than intellectual distinction). Studies of such topics are needed.

According to Paul Dressel's *Handbook of Academic Evaluation* (1976), the president's responsibility is to lead the institution toward change consistent with stated goals and values. Dressel is less nihilistic about college and university administration than Cohen and March. Yet he believes that the modern president can no longer exercise power but must achieve change through compromise, leading toward general objectives without stifling individuals or groups.

Books about the search for a college or university president, such as Joseph F. Kauffman's *The Selection of College and University Presidents* (1974), note the new pressures on college presidents—for sound management and accountability, and, in public colleges, for political leadership—that equal or exceed pressures for educational innovation. Kauffman notes the decline and illusoriness of support for the president concerning whatever educational change is possible.

Kauffman's most recent book, *At the Pleasure of the Board* (1980), explores more fully the need for trustees who will support a president and the need for presidents who have a clearer view of what they can do with proper support, with the emphasis on the former. Perhaps presidents are inclined, because of professional isolation, to dramatize their trials and the chances to be misunderstood. Faculty members are aware that this attitude is popular among presidents. They are also aware that most presidents love their jobs and would fight to the last ditch to keep them.

Articles by Herbert J. Walberg and Joseph C. Burke have noted the increasing pressures on the college president to be a manager. In "The Academic President: Colleague, Administrator, or Spokesman?" (1969), Walberg calculates the amount of time presidents spend on various activities and concludes that they are primarily administrators of bureaucracies. Burke calls on the president to be an education leader despite competing pressures, to remind constituents of the institution's purpose, and to create an atmosphere in which all can pursue that purpose ("Coping with the Role of College or University President," 1977). In "The College Presidency: Life Between a Rock and a Hard Place" (1979), Theodore Hesburgh, discussing the difficulties of the presidency, still assumes that the president's role is to have a personal vision and to get the best people to share and help achieve it.

Perhaps the most persistent difficulty in studying college presidents as education leaders is the dehumanizing influence of their modern role as managers of a chronically underdefined social organi-

zation. Between 1969 and 1973, that role was underscored by Earl
Cheit (*The New Depression in Higher Education*, 1971), Hans Jenny,
Walter Jellema, Frederick Balderston, Victor Baldridge, Ben
Lawrence, and other specialists in higher education systems management. All but a handful of presidents were forced to deal with the
burdens of budgets and fund raising, and this forced preoccupation
lent credence to popular conclusions that higher education administration would soon be, if it was not already, indistinguishable from the
management of any highly skilled, labor-intensive organization.

Faculty unionization in the 1970s all but ended the separation
between the college presidency and outright management. Books and
articles were written about how to select a college president capable
of carrying out the new management imperatives while looking,
speaking, and, if possible, acting like the leader of a community of
scholars. Service organizations such as the National Center for Higher
Education Management Systems (NCHEMS), in Boulder, Colorado,
grew apace while references to business methods (MBO, PPBS, MIS,
and so forth) regularly cropped up during administrative cabinet
meetings. At various institutions at various times, the abandonment of
academic collegiality in favor of getting the college's business finished
has threatened to become complete.

A few stubborn facts about academe have stood in the way. One is
the custom of playing down on campus anything that smacks of
mechanization in the educative process. The enormous growth of
electronic data processing has not changed the faculty's perception of
the educative process. In the university, where for a thousand years
professors have treated their associates as peers no matter what the
relative seniority or status may be, there persists a common distaste
for using terms suggesting employer-employee relations. Faculty
members resolutely decline to speak of higher learning as something
that can be managed. The president and his cabinet officers may
manage the institution so that the blackboard trays have chalk and
that faculty members can find a place to park their cars. But the credo
is that administrators do not—they cannot—manage the professors.

In *The Managerial Revolution in Higher Education* (1966),
Francis Rourke and Glenn Brooks appeal to faculty members to grasp
their necessary role in the change toward a more complex government of institutions:

> The necessity for shifting from direct democracy to representative
> government is not always recognized by university faculties, how-
> ever. The most paradoxical development in higher education in

recent years has been the fact that the status of the individual faculty member has been growing on university campuses even while his participation in university government has been declining. In the old days the faculty asserted itself by claiming the right to participate in university government. Now, however, there are bigger fish for the academic man to fry on many campuses— research contracts, consultantships, and the other spoils of the affluent academic society. If anything, the individual faculty member now tends to assert his power by declining to participate in university government. Unless effective channels for representing the views of the faculty in university government are maintained, however, control over internal academic policy will be left entirely in the hands of business administrators. This trend will follow not from administrative design or aggrandizement, but as a result of faculty default. From the point of view of the efficiency of the university, this will be a highly undesirable development, not because it violates any inalienable right of the faculty to control academic affairs, but simply because on academic matters faculty advice is essential to the development of relevant university policy.[3]

Where does this statement leave the college president who must manage the institution yet who is still called to lead an organization dedicated to higher learning? Some presidents have given up all but the exterior, ceremonial aspects of the academic function. Others try to act like educators, only to find themselves rebuffed by academic powers in order to stay on top of academic policy. Most presidents struggle for a compromise position between manager and education leader, a position that, because of the financial problems weighing on the school, becomes harder to maintain every year.

Much is written about this issue, indicating that it remains a live question. Summer conferences on how to be a "real college president in these times" are being held nationwide. A spring 1980 issue of the *Chronicle of Higher Education* listed thirteen such conferences scheduled for that summer; eight listed management problems as their agenda, while only three centered on college instruction.

In the transcripts of the interviews on which the following chapters are based, faculty members and students on the majority of campuses frequently appraised their president as "mainly a manager." In four of the twenty-five visits, the appraisal was yet more direct: "He (or she) is mainly a public relations person" or, blunter still, "a politician." Such judgments are scarcely calculated to increase

3. Francis E. Rourke and Glenn E. Brooks, *The Managerial Revolution in Higher Education* (Baltimore: The Johns Hopkins University Press, 1966).

the president's amour propre as he or she leads the hooded procession on commencement day.

The present writers feel that a more analytical approach to the human dynamics of the college presidency is needed. This book examines the place of executive leadership in institutions of higher education in the 1980s. The report, derived from the Presidency Project, has been drawn from conversations with presidents as they reviewed their prospects for providing intellectual growth, in the broadest cognitive sense, for students, professors, and professional specialists—in short, for every person associated with the institution.

This notion of fostering intellectual growth can quickly become vainglorious in the actual setting. Yet without some vision of what a college or university as a whole can achieve, the chief executive is left with little to think about besides the annual cycle of planning, budget making, programs, and evaluation. Such work is often easier to accomplish in organizations other than colleges and universities, and the salary is usually better.

The cumulative effect of current books and articles on the college presidency seems, on the whole, a discouraging one for readers. When taking office, a president pledges a great deal, but the life that ensues appears mainly distinguished by negatives. Still, new presidents continue to be sought. Whatever the status of the institution, small and local or world-renowned, a new presidency is a major event.

Two channels appear to open before the observer of institutional leadership in higher education. One puts the president amid a stream of forces that stress the limitations of time, energy, funds, and a persistently vexing sociology for those who would seek to lead. The total effect of the leadership game is seen as essentially zero, even though changes do occur and institutions, through some planetary force perhaps too subtle for analysis, do move forward.

The other channel reflects the belief that the presidency, with all its defects and inherent obstacles, retains a power to move an institution in a chosen direction. The situation reflects an assumption that leadership motives of presidents, whatever their outcomes, are more likely to be constructive than otherwise. One result may indeed be failure, but that can happen in any organization.

The study question then becomes, What do presidents make out of their office that keeps it dynamic in many, if not most, institutions? Can a president learn to lead, or, at least, not to settle for the zero-sum game? The balance of this book presents findings along the course of the second channel of presidential leadership.

2 The President: Leader, Parent, Hero, Villain

Three Major Results

Several outstanding results emerge from an analysis of the Presidency Project interviews. First, the president *does* make a difference. In line with the thesis of this book, our data do not support the view, held by some observers, that institutions can run themselves and that the president is something of a figurehead.

Second, the job requires an enormous expenditure of time and energy. It entails handling many different kinds of responsibilities during the same day and often results in the blurring of the president's public and private life. It requires friendliness, the constant giving of self, and responsiveness to the demand that the president be a nice person—an emotional expenditure that makes scant allowance for the depressions and withdrawals that are part of the daily lives of ordinary persons.

Third, even though one of the president's primary tasks is dealing with the economic problems, he or she rarely concentrates only on the budgetary and political aspects of the role. Most presidents also aspire to be leaders in education as well.

This chapter deals with the interpersonal aspects of presidential leadership, describing how presidents communicate and interact with their constituencies, how they involve or do not involve their administrative colleagues and faculty in the decision-making process, and how they respond to the rational and less rational expectations of their office.

The President's Entourage

The most important fact about the president is that he or she makes the decisions. Every administrator interviewed—vice presidents, provosts, and deans—reported that, at some point, they disagreed with the president's stand on an issue. But the president's word prevails. Moreover, when it is known that the president's position on certain matters is firm, many issues are not raised or are raised differently than if his or her preferences are not known. Presidents vary in flexibility, and, accordingly, their subordinate administrators may influence to a greater or lesser degree the decision-making process. But the president's stance, personality, and bias can affect such questions as recruitment policies, faculty selection and promotion, curricular programs, and student services.

An immediate lesson from our study is that presidents vary in the way they make decisions. This variability is a result of several factors. First, each president has a unique personality as well as certain idiosyncrasies. Second, the process of arriving at conclusions is restricted by the nature of the president's relationships with others who participate in making decisions; authority and rank do count for something. Third, deliberative procedures—either because they are not sophisticated enough or rational enough—often do not help achieve an optimal solution.

A remarkable feature of the institutions we studied is that the administrators who are second and third in command almost always have a special respect and admiration—even affection—for their president. "Hero worship" would be too strong a term to describe this relationship, but our data reveal that they consider the president a superior person. This admiration may be due partly, but not wholly, to the fact that often the president selects these administrators. A more decisive factor may be that the president's role and personality encourage this kind of attitude in his or her close colleagues. By contrast, persons further removed from the president's immediate entourage tend to be more critical of the president. First, constituents who are at a distance from the president—especially faculty members—often represent interests that, realistically or in imagination, are adversarial. Second, these constituents are susceptible to stereotypical notions of the arbitrariness and impersonality of power, and at times these notions replace a charismatic loyalty to the president. For instance, the provost of one institution in our sample described his president as a "true intellectual, good administrator, and a humanitarian" but reported with surprise that "some of the faculty members out there think that he is cold at times. I don't think they know the man, because he has always put the faculty before any other constituency on campus."[1]

1. Unless otherwise documented, quotations are from transcripts of the Presidency Project.

The people in the president's immediate environment are on the same team. They have a much keener sense of the president's options than do persons further removed from the president. Moreover, they are usually more oriented toward the institution as a whole as distinguished from specific department or student interests. The fact that they share a common purpose and have greater access to information means that they have a different orientation to the president. Interestingly enough, this bond serves to counter their possible personal ambitions for becoming chief executive. The people immediately surrounding the president give few indications of great mental distance from the president or of scheming against him or her.

Nevertheless, the process of deliberation among the upper echelon often leaves much to be desired. Styles vary. Some presidents are more comfortable working with individuals, while others prefer to work with groups. Although most provosts or vice presidents reported success in occasionally influencing the president's thinking, they usually seemed to work through accommodation. That they concur with the president's approach may be the reason they were selected by the president and the reason they stay in office.

The President's Relations with Faculty and Students

The top-level deliberative process at most institutions, then, could be more creative; perhaps it is less so because of "compulsive" priorities dictated by events, e.g., budgetary retrenchment. The process of deliberation, however, functions even less well in regard to the institution as a whole. Our interviews reveal a glaring lack of consultation with both faculty members and students in areas that vitally affect their well-being. Faculty members and students may be informed of startling news—announcements of the elimination of programs or an increase in tuition, for instance—without sufficient prior consultation or psychological preparation. Presidents often say that they made glaring mistakes in their earlier years and that they have learned from them. But lack of experience is probably too simple an explanation.

Our data indicate that the problem lies not only, and perhaps not primarily, in the president's lack of experience but rather in the structure of relationships between the president and his or her constituency. The problem begins with the division of interests—i.e., when the faculty represents special interests and the president represents the well-being of the institution as a whole. The division is made more profound by the difference in the experiences of faculty members and presidents. A faculty member's life centers on the classroom, the library, and the laboratory; a president's life centers on management and public relations. The gap becomes even larger because opportunities for working together are inadequate. The contacts between faculty members and the president—the political context of faculty meetings, the formalized context of committee work, or semirelaxed socializing—do not provide genuine opportunities for working together. Moreover, particularly since the 1970s, the president has been driven to make decisions that bring inevitable hurt to faculty or that require of students greater financial outlays or other discomforts. The president's options often are limited, and somebody—often the president—must personify institutional decisions that may seem more arbitrary than they are.

It is no wonder that some presidents, in their weaker moments, say that they wish universities and colleges were like business corporations, in which decisions are made hierarchically. These presidents are quick to add—they would not have lasted long as presidents if they thought differently—that they understand that a college or university is a collegial institution and that the faculty has precedence in making curricular decisions.

Most presidents are skilled in working with people, and these interpersonal skills, which are usually more than public relations manipulation, can throw a gloss over disharmonies. The president is usually a genuinely effusive person who likes others and wants to be liked by them. He or she usually has a sense of humor and a capacity for the quick personal remark that can make even a casual encounter with a student or faculty member memorable for them. As one student said of his president: "He doesn't put on a show; he really does enjoy his job. Sometimes he is in a rush, so he will just say, 'hello.' He has a good memory for names. He even knows who I am."

Given the many constituents a president has to please, not only persons on campus but outsiders as well, no one should even consider taking on such a position unless he or she has more than an ordinary amount of charm. And many presidents do. One faculty member described his president thus: "His interpersonal relations are fantastic. I am absolutely amazed by the number of people he knows and the number of things he knows about them. He has a personal charm and ability to speak for the institution that makes people much happier about giving money. People probably follow him around, saying, 'Could you use some money?' "

At the same time, presidents are often sensitive and vulnerable. Their position is an eminent one. They have to make hard decisions, and, almost by necessity, they have to keep their distance from people on campus (for example, being too closely involved with faculty members might make personnel decisions even harder). Consequently, an outsider might think that presidents would be rather thick-skinned. But their tendency to like people and to be liked, as well as their need to do good to others and to be admired by them, indicates that they are not exactly hard-boiled.

Some persons may be attracted to the job of president because of the opportunity of enlarging the circle of people for whom they are important. The need to be liked may account for the special sensitivity that several close collaborators said characterizes their president. This need may also help explain the reported tendency of some presidents to grant favors to people who seek them out, even if the favors are granted at the expense of the authority of subordinates in whose domain the request falls.

Another consequence of the need to be liked is the increasing accumulation of disappointments. Most presidents begin their term with a honeymoon period, but soon they suffer many frustrations or defeats. Inevitably, they make enemies. Moreover, they are subject to a style of attack in the student press and among faculty that would not be tolerated for other persons. In recent years, calls for the resignation or firing of presidents have been made with growing liberality and with lesser provocation.

As a result, presidents who have been in office for a long time tend to insulate themselves from contacts with the outside world. One president, at the beginning of his term, saw himself as a friend of the students. In the difficult period of nationwide student unrest, he spent hours with the students at his institution and was able to gain their confidence. A few years later, after some students had unearthed secret documents about the president's allocation of funds and voiced strong criticism of his administration, the president would no longer see representatives of the student press. This case exemplifies the famous maxim, from Plato's *Republic*, that leaders of the people, at the beginning of their rule, are generally regarded as the people's friends but, as their time in office wears on, increasingly have to guard themselves against the real or supposed enmity of the people they are meant to serve.

Almost every president's approach to governing has some procedural flaws. Some presidents have difficulty delegating authority;

hence, their days are swamped with attention to details that would best be left to others. Further, in spite of the enormous pressures on them, they often seem to be unable to budget their time. For instance, some presidents see many people who could be seen by other representatives of the institution; also the amount of time spent in these visits does not always seem to be warranted. Communications to immediate associates, not to mention those to faculty members or students, are often poor. Several presidents in our sample had suffered major defeats because they had failed to consult with or notify faculty members about actions that deeply affected their welfare. In one instance, a decision that ought to have come from the board of trustees was announced by the president just before the board's meeting. Another president forestalled a faculty group's anticipated recommendations for the committee appointment of a faculty member he did not like by changing the description of the position to be filled; he thus avoided having to turn down the recommendation directly. A faculty member close to the president described this maneuver as smart politics, but such transparent manipulation is likely to alienate people. A more damaging tactic is to pretend that meetings with staff members or other groups are meetings for discussing issues and seeking advice when the real purpose is either to manipulate the group or merely to pretend to consult them.

The flaws mentioned here are remediable flaws. Sophistication in administration, like sophistication in teaching, is for almost every president an acquired art, an art that can be further cultivated. The presidents in our sample have often shown great sagacity in exercising their art. Many of them act on the principle that their powers are limited unless they have "lieutenants" among the faculty and students. These presidents said that they had kept a low profile in many important enterprises; they had talked indefatigably with many individual faculty members until a plan emerged that faculty believed in, thought of as their own, and were willing to persuade their colleagues to accept.

Some tactics for achieving cooperation can be astute, such as those used by a president who wished to help bring about a major curricular change. He realized that meeting the faculty on a department-by-department basis was likely to encourage particularism and maintain the status quo, so he decided to make sure that each group he met with was composed of persons from different departments. Thus, this approach was oriented more to the university as a whole.

Presidents are usually very energetic in pursuing information, and they generally seem to have a large array of facts at their command.

To keep abreast of what is happening on campus, they sometimes greatly change the basic data-gathering system of their institution. The president may be the most broadly informed person in the entire institution. Unfortunately, this breadth of information at times segregates presidents from faculty members and students, whose information is often limited and oriented to their own turf.

The administrative styles of presidents vary. Some are more directive than others. Many presidents in our sample have learned not to worry about who gets credit for the successful resolution of an issue; they have learned to work through and with other people. Yet these same presidents can also describe themselves as favoring a more interventionist leadership style. One president enthusiastically described an intervention: "The faculty members had wrestled with an educational problem for the third time in a faculty meeting. Finally the president said quietly but forcefully, 'If you cannot resolve this issue among you, I will resolve it for you.' At that moment the debate took on a different tone."

Presidents have to make decisions—many decisions—and often with little time to think about issues involved. One administrator complained that his president only needs "about 10 percent of the data to make a decision; once he makes the decision, he stands by it." The same president is described by another administrator as one who takes the initiative: "He initiates ideas, proposals, and policies. The administrative style of some presidents consists merely of reacting to proposals that are presented to them, but that kind of presidency is disastrous." But to a faculty member who chairs a major committee, this president's decisiveness goes too far. He describes the president as "authoritarian," adding that "this president's desires will prevail. He imposes his will on others." Which of these three perceptions is accurate? Possibly all three, and this ambiguity is an indication of the difficulty of the president's job.

The tasks of the presidency call for decisiveness and action, and most persons who make their way into that office seem to have the requisite personality characteristics. Yet at the same time, as already suggested, many of them exhibit behavior patterns usually associated with shy people. Many of the persons we interviewed described their president as thin-skinned, afraid of the faculty, very private, and unable to take criticism easily.

In addition, the nature of the job tends to isolate the president from people. Presidents complain about not having any close friends. When they talk, people hear not the individual but "the president." Their closest friends may be other presidents, with whom they can relax and commiserate. The constant battles with constituents and the repetition of complaints and issues can be wearing. Finding means of regeneration is difficult, and the president's isolation makes regeneration even more difficult. Moreover, the people around the president tend to "filter" through the sieve of their self-interest whatever they tell him or her. Every college and university president needs what Franklin Delano Roosevelt had—a Harry Hopkins to speak truth to power in a relaxed and friendly fashion, and an Eleanor Roosevelt to help the president hear and perceive what he or she cannot be told or see directly. In addition, the tensions of the job need to be discussed more fully so that better ways of coping with them can be found. In that regard every president needs a "psychiatrist," that is, a person with whom the president can sort out the emotional burdens of the job.

The president's style and accomplishments stamp the institution in a special way, and most presidents deeply desire to leave a mark of their individuality. To that end, a president may propose new plans or new solutions to institutional problems—selectivity in favor of more able students, a fresh master plan for general education, the adoption of new programs or procedures—a women's studies program, a managerial training program, collective bargaining—or the abolition of established programs—a master's program, collective bargaining. Some projects, however, are clearly forced on the president. Today most presidents must wrestle with the problems of achieving financial solvency. Some favor economizing—for example, reducing the faculty and administrative staff. Others work to increase enrollment, hoping to generate income in this way. The options for increasing enrollment, for instance, are limited—only in some circumstances can vigorous recruitment increase the number of students, and then only in institutions in which the costs of new facilities do not outweigh the benefits of increased enrollment. Presidents can also express their individuality through "pet" projects, which allow them more freedom of choice. These are often perfectly respectable projects, such as the gerontological center at one institution in our sample, which would not have come into existence unless the president had a special interest in it and was instrumental in gathering faculty support and raising funds.

Many projects through which presidents leave their personal mark on an institution are neither those that are forced on them by external circumstances nor those that they freely assume. These projects constitute a response to fiscal, ideological, educational, and administrative necessities but at the same time allow room for creativity. One college in our sample provides a notable example of this kind of approach. This particular institution increased its size and income and, at the same time, introduced genuine educational innovations through a combination of measures—by going coeducational, by adopting a new college calendar, by requiring attendance for one summer term, by using study facilities abroad and in other parts of this country, and by computerizing the system of record keeping.

When presidents retrench—for example, when they abolish a particular department or program—they are perceived by faculty members as being callous and business-minded, with little understanding of scholarship. These perceptions have their source in the fact that faculty's work is almost entirely identified with their specialty; hence they are extremely sensitive to anything that threatens its continuing practice. Yet specialty work is only one way to cultivate the intellect, to further critical and productive thinking, and the president may have educational alternatives in mind. Many theorists—for instance, Earl McGrath, in *The Graduate School and the Decline of Liberal Learning* (1959)—have raised questions about the fit between specialty learning and students' general education.

Still, the faculty's complaints may not be as self-interested as they seem. Most presidents have been away from the classroom for a long time, and the intricacies of the intellectual pursuit may have become dim. Some faculty members interviewed said that they wished the president would occasionally teach a course. (Some presidents do continue to teach.) This demand may be a legitimate one, for the president would then have a more solid base for participating in curricular decision making.

Retrenchment is a threat to faculty security and morale, and presidents differ in the amount of care they devote to the human aspects of retrenchment. Clearly, during retrenchment of any kind, the personal and career interests of faculty members should be paramount considerations for the president, if only for the sake of the faculty members who will be retained.

The President as Parent

The discussion thus far has centered on the relatively rational terrain of presidential leadership and management. Now, however, the focus is on a more mysterious, more emotional realm. The interviews indicate that at nearly all institutions the president is a paternal figure. Like any father, he is expected to be home more often, to pay more attention to the "children," to say more kind words, to know what his family is doing, to be interested in what they are doing, and to be ready with money when it is needed. Often he is perceived to be able to give more than he does, and he is usually considered to be more powerful than he really is. Some considerable effort of his may be taken for granted. One president described his experiences after obtaining for his faculty the largest salary increase ever given. Not one person said to him, "Hey, that was nice of you."

The university is often viewed as a family, and the president is expected to be a charismatic, all-knowing, all-good father. Not only do students demonstrate this longing, but so do supposedly more mature faculty members and administrators. Perhaps the purpose of education should be to divest the public of these magical expectations of its leaders. Such expectations bedevil Americans also in the area of national politics, where critical assessments of presidential candidates may be outweighed by the image and illusion of a good father. At times the president can turn these expectations to his advantage—for example, in resolving a dispute or collecting money. A mayor of a midwestern town once said that the only power a mayor has resides in the fact that people believe he has power. The same could be said of the college or university president.

Clark Kerr, in *The Uses of the University* (1963) has brilliantly described the president's job as one that is an almost impossible conglomeration of roles. In addition to the on-campus roles already discussed, the president has much work to do off campus: he or she is the institution's representative to the public, legislators, alumni, and trustees. Some institutions even desire their president to play a national role; their motives include enhancing the institution's status and sharing with the nation their leader's competence and charisma.

The persons interviewed at the institutions in our sample usually conceded that the president had to spend a considerable amount of time away from campus. Most agreed that this public relations work was an important service for the institution because, among other things, it helped raise funds for the institution. Although constituents could understand the president's absence, many felt a sense of loss. Often when faculty members said they wished the president were more of a scholar or more interested in scholarship, they were really saying that they wanted their president to pay more attention to the academic side of the institution.

Yet how can one person handle the president's responsibilities on and off campus? Do not the requirements of the presidency provide a preeminent example of what the sociologists call role strain? Potential donors want the president to solicit them before they make a contribution to the institution. Faculty members want to be recognized by the president for their excellent teaching or research skills. Students want to see the president more often in the dormitory, in the cafeteria, or at some classroom or curricular event. Yet how is one person to fulfill all these demands? Here again, a deep-seated paternalism and orientation toward "one father" make the job of the presidency very difficult. What is remarkable is that the job is done at all and with as much energy, persistence, inventiveness, and even brilliance.

The job is also draining and self-consuming. As one president put it: "There are the inevitable responsibilities of fund raising, of external relationships (including relationships with the alumni), of business functions, of the relationship to the governing body, all of which tend to focus on the president. To avoid having all one's time consumed by what are essentially nonacademic matters requires a tremendous effort. These issues usually are not central to the academic objectives of the university, but they are a very important part of the process of achieving these objectives." Nevertheless, in spite of the fatiguing and even exhausting aspects of the job, power and position can be great stimulants, as the health and longevity of top executives seem to corroborate.

Constituency Participation and Leadership

Two final comments should be made about the issues discussed in this chapter. First, examining the data institution by institution revealed that any single statement when taken by itself alone, whether made by a president or by other persons interviewed was rather one-sided. With further research the data became not only richer but considerably more revealing. The comments of members of different constituencies indicated mistakes in presidential procedure and objectives as well as accomplishments. Particularly astonishing was the good sense, often good managerial sense, shown by the students. Students supposedly have only a worm's eye view, yet they were often capable of statesmanlike assessment.

The data made increasingly clear that many persons at these institutions had valuable insights about the presidency but that these insights were squandered because the various people and constituents were isolated from one another. If all this wisdom could be made to flow together, if all these insights could cooperatively be directed toward the assessment of institutional problems, institutions might function better and would be happier places. One president inter-viewed had fostered the policy that his administration would have no secrets. This approach represented an important step toward institu-tional coherence, for it undercut paranoia and maneuvering and laid the groundwork for understanding the decisions—even the painful ones—that had to be made.

The concept of participatory democracy in colleges and universi-ties is no longer fashionable, just as the German concept of the *Gruppenuniversitat*, popular in the late 1960s, is now out of use. But the principle of participatory democracy is a good one, as long as it is taken to mean a consultative model rather than a rigidly parliamen-tary one. The use of collective wisdom, with a new name, is perhaps an idea worth reviving.

A second comment: The Presidency Project was concerned with the question of whether the president is a leader or a manager. The data clearly show that whether presidents wish it or not—and usually they wish it—they are leaders. Given the organizational structure of the university, which is undergirded by the parentalism just described, the president affects curriculum, department structures, and student life and services. He or she affects not only substance and structure but also the institution's morale and ambiance. The mood or spirit of the institution is important because it determines the zest with which the institution and its people carry on their business; hence it can either release or inhibit energies and set the outlook toward the future. The institution's mood, through its effect on the students, indirectly helps determine the self-confidence of society as a whole. The ques-tion is not whether the president is a leader or a manager, but what kind of a leader he or she is.

The presidents interviewed were deeply concerned about the budget—the raising and distribution of money. Some constituents want the president to be a glorified development officer, bringing home the money and asking few questions about how it is used. However, the president's pivotal relation to money also puts him or her in a crucial position to affect many other institutional issues. The salient variables are to what extent the president's money-seeking activities are informed by educational considerations and what these considerations are.

Our data show that presidents are leaders. They might be better leaders if they more fully recognize their function in all its ramifica-tions, if they realize that they need more education—that is, constant reflection on their office, appropriate regular evaluation, and whatever in-service "training" is available. Moreover, they should be mindful of Dos Passos's suggestion that *democratic* leaders have the responsibility to make their followers less, not more, dependent on them.

The alternating moods, the sense of achievement, and the sadness of the presidency can best be summed up in the words of one president in our sample. He said that being a president is like being a tennis ball that is served and batted around during a game. Some days he asks himself: " What is going to happen to me today? Is this what a leader ought to be doing—bouncing back and forth from issue to issue?" In spite of these feelings, however, he holds on to another vision of the presidency: "My task is always to be a leader, not just holding my finger in the wind and saying, Where does everyone want to go? My task is to plant the seeds of some ideas with people and to watch to see which ones are growing and moving and taking life. My task is responsive interaction with people."

3 The President in the Academic Community

The preceding chapter focused on the structure of the president's relationships with his or her constituency. Also discussed were the differences between the president's interests and experiences and the faculty's interests and experiences—differences that can divide them. Presidents are oriented toward the institution as a whole, whereas faculty members are oriented toward their department. The president's activities center on management and public relations, the faculty's on teaching and research. This structure allows little opportunity for the president and faculty to work together, and the gap widens as the president makes decisions "that bring inevitable hurt to the faculty."

Although some presidents and faculty members who were interviewed managed to transcend these structural barriers to a considerable degree, much of the testimony reflected a sense of alienation, as well as a sense of regret for the lack of understanding. Each side thought that it understood the other but that the other did not understand *it*, as excerpts from interviews at the same institution illustrate:

PRESIDENT: If a president puts out his or her entire agenda, people's energies are addressed to criticism. Not necessarily negative criticism, but academics are trained to theorize and criticize. That's what the academic mind is all about.

FACULTY MEMBER: Coming up through the ranks teaches you something about the gut nature, the innate second nature, of academics that nobody outside will ever understand. The president can say things that may be important and accurate, but she just doesn't display enough understanding of the inner workings of the academic mind.

The generalizations presidents and faculty members make about each other reflect in part their differing roles and professional interests but also suggest that these two groups see each other as inherently alien beings. Presidents felt that faculty members as individuals have

22

exciting ideas but as a group suffer from inertia; they have too many different viewpoints, talk too much, and never agree. Their satisfactions are intellectual and do not depend on practical achievement. They are oblivious to demographic and environmental changes that put economic constraints on programs. They focus only on their own scholarship and have little concern for students' personal development or for institutional matters outside their discipline. Attitudes like these have led some presidents we interviewed to make decisions without consulting faculty members and to manipulate them into going along with a policy without assenting to its full implications.

Faculty members, on the other hand, said presidents think about education issues only from the financial point of view and will not take reasonable risks for the sake of educational innovation. They always side with the board of trustees. They are not true academicians, do not have time to think about educational philosophy, and do not worry (or worry sufficiently) about having the time. They enjoy being administrators; administration excites them. One faculty member said of her president, "That's what he likes to do and what he has liked to do from the very first." The implication of the faculty members' attitudes is that the best administrator is a reluctant one—a curious attitude for professionals who stand to benefit from an inspired administration of their institution.

Characteristics of Individual Presidents

Faculty members nevertheless welcomed some presidents into the academic community; others they invited grudgingly, and some they excluded. Characteristics that enhanced a president's likelihood of being accepted included a Ph.D. in an academic field; experience in teaching; experience in academic administration; and a style that projects an intellectual rather than a managerial image. Approximately 80 percent of the presidents in our study met the first three criteria. Some who had not come into office from faculty ranks or from the administrative staff of that particular institution were considered outsiders; they were perceived as not understanding the institution's character or the value of a particular faculty member or program or of not having a grasp of details of the curriculum. If such a president attempted to introduce a nontraditional program or fired a popular professor or administrator, the perception of misunderstanding was strengthened, particularly if he or she acted in an authoritarian manner.

Presidents who came directly or indirectly from careers in politics or public administration were suspect. Constituents questioned whether their interests, attitudes, and ambitions were educationally oriented.

Characteristics of Individual Institutions

Our sample showed that characteristics of particular institutions influenced but did not determine the president's relationship to the faculty. One president stated that at his institution the president traditionally played a central role in formulating education policy, so his participation in the academic realm was not seen as intrusion. Resources were relatively plentiful, and because he was not constantly preoccupied with raising money and struggling with the budget, he was perceived as more of an academician.

Another college had recently fired a president, and antiadministration feelings were strong. The incoming president, in order to lessen distrust between the faculty and the administration, appointed faculty members to all administrative positions except that of treasurer. He also made sure his consultation with the faculty about education policy matters was conspicuous.

If the selection of a president is a compromise or a controversial choice, some faculty members will feel that this person has been imposed on them. The president will have to come to terms with these faculty members, perhaps, as one president did, by appointing a chief academic officer who would be acceptable to the faculty and who would be responsible for academic operation. This president had an easy relationship with the faculty members, even though—or perhaps because—he remained on the fringe of their community.

Efforts toward Understanding

Despite these alienating attitudes, whether preconceived or based on experience, presidents and their constituents express a desire for mutual understanding and support. Presidents expect resistance to their education proposals but want to feel that they are, in some sense, comrades of the faculty members. Their expressions of emotional isolation are poignant:

> I have faced demonstrations each of five of the last six springs around here, and I have walked through and by demonstrations in front of this building. Not easy affairs. I have gone over to the faculty club and have had faculty members tell me, "Well, that's your job."

There's a kind of isolation despite all the collegiality I've told you about. Someone may ask, "Well, what do you think, what do you really think about it?" And then you say what you think, and you realize he didn't hear you; he heard "the president."

Constituents likewise want the president to know what being in their position is like. Faculty members would like the president to publish so that he or she would understand the difficulties of scholarship. Speaking wistfully of a president who taught during the early years of his presidency, a faculty member said, "He was delightful when he was teaching; he saw the problems with the students. If he could just teach a course, even every other year, then the faculty would feel a little bit more collegially toward him.

A student remarked that presidents have forgotten what being a student is like and suggested that if a president had college-age children, he or she would be conscious of the problems of young people. If the president cannot or does not teach, and most do not, he or she can sometimes achieve some degree of comradeship with the faculty members by allowing them to participate in the administration (as deans or provosts) or in governance bodies. One president reported that this approach allows faculty members to see issues from an administrative point of view, and the chasm is reduced: "Frequently a problem is a problem because it has no ideal solution, not because no one has ever thought about the problem. This concept is hard for nonparticipants to grasp." A faculty senate member noted that "the president is not the only agent on the financial front; we have to probe financial issues too."

An active student government member at a state university where students have an unusually effective role in governance identifies with the president's concern for external responsibilities, a part of the president's job that often alienates him or her from the academic community:

> Recently I have been receiving criticism from fellow students because I have been spending a lot of time off campus with outside agencies such as the board of regents, the state legislature, a foundation, and the alumni association. I find that the president is very active in these same agencies, and by paralleling my problems with his, I can see the necessity for his role outside the university.

Such intermingling of administrative and academic functions can alleviate but not eliminate the gulf between the faculty and the president. The gulf is especially conspicuous during periods of litigation involving the faculty and the president. One president remarked: "The administration and the faculty are distinguishable bodies, even when, as in our case, some members of the administration are also faculty members. The line is drawn. There is so much hostility now to the administration, for a variety of reasons, that administrators must maintain that common front."

Faculty members, too, feel obliged to maintain a "common front," even at institutions where there is no marked hostility between the faculty and the administration. A president who has hosted a few faculty senate meetings at his home noted, "The senate members wouldn't want to meet here very often, because the impression would be that they were being bought off. So the meetings are always at their place." A faculty member at that institution backed off from saying that the senate tends to "support" the president: "That sounds like we're lackeys for the administration." Faculty members also resent their decreasing control over curriculum that is formulated by a college senate, which includes members of the administration, rather than a faculty senate.

The President's Decision-Making Power

At the root of the president's adversarial relationship with the faculty is the fact that the president has more power than any other person in the institution. A faculty member, speaking of the differences between administrators and faculty members, said that administrators "do not get excited by ideas." Another commented that "administrators must make decisions." An academic administrator, discussing the conventional roles that presidents get locked into, connected those two attributes:

> I like to play with ideas. I like to toss something out and argue it with myself. The problem with being an administrator is that people don't understand that your purpose is to play with an idea. When people perceive you as having power, they can't deal with you at the suggestive level. It's hard to be an intellectual and an administrator.

Furthermore, admitted a president quoted earlier, presidents do not always reveal to faculty members their complete policy agendas. Another president conceded that he did not reveal his full motivation for a particular proposal. Thus, even when presidents are occupied with issues that the faculty feels presidents should be concerned with, they may arouse suspicion.

A president who wanted to initiate an inventory of academic programs for purposes of long-range planning sensed the faculty's suspicion that the project was "a budgetary device." Another president proposed a program in which professionals in business and government would visit the classes, thus underscoring for the students the relationship between a liberal arts education and the outside world; however, the suggested program was perceived as "one more mechanism for looking over the shoulders of faculty members to see how well they're doing." A third president said he is isolated from the early stages of search procedures for deans because search committees are sometimes suspicious of a president's motives.

Nevertheless, presidents manage to achieve many policy goals to which they give a high priority. The academic inventory referred to is underway; the program of visiting committees, after a two-year delay (during which it gained faculty support), has made a modest beginning; and if presidents are isolated from early stages of search procedures, they are influential in later ones. Thus, while presidents intent on improving the quality of education at their institutions are perplexed at the faculty's suspicion of their motives, faculty members have some justification for closely scrutinizing the presidents' proposals.

Tensions inherent in the president-faculty relationship are eased by a sense of empathy which can grow from a combination of factors, including the characteristics of president and institution already discussed. The following cases illustrate ways in which that empathy, or the lack of it, can affect the president's influence on the college or university.

The Spectrum: From Alienation to Identification

In our sample, the faculty members' attitudes toward the president and the presidents' attitudes toward faculty members ranged from severe alienation to close identification.

Faculty members at one institution felt extremely alienated from their president because of his professional background and administrative style. Although he had spent most of his professional life in a university and had once taught at the institution of which he had become president, he had been a member of a professional faculty and, therefore, "was an outsider as far as the arts and sciences faculty was concerned." (He was, however, considered an academic peer by members of the professional faculty. This situation will be discussed later.) An academic administrator there said it took the president a long time to get a sense of the university as a whole and that he never was able to empathize with certain programs.

The faculty members, nevertheless, praised this president for his intelligence, his analytical and organizational ability, his skill in directing discussions in council sessions, and his sensitivity in dealing with colleagues. They even credited him with being the kind of president the institution needed: "We needed a superb manager, and he was one; he was brilliant."

His management expertise and the measures he took to make the institution more efficient, however, further distanced him from faculty members who already felt alienated by his background:

> He had a much better sense of our jeopardy than most faculty members. He wanted to make us more efficient, so he gave a lot of emphasis to nonacademic staff, which has never been the priority of academicians, of course. His style in general gave him the image of a large corporation president, an ideal technocrat who could do everything well. He did do everything well; but because he attempted to do so much, he had no personal impact at all on most of the faculty members.

The image of corporate manager was especially damaging to this president because it contrasted with that of his predecessor, "an old club guy, a nice relaxed humanities professor," who had been thought of as the faculty members' leader.

At the time of our interview this president had resigned, and his successor had been chosen. Referring to the search process, a faculty member said, "They had to get somebody who could run the shop—and it is a complicated one—but they wanted one of us; that is, first of all, it had to be one of us." The president-to-be is a former administrator and member of the arts and sciences faculty at that institution. According to an associate, he will "walk into his office almost loved by an extraordinary range of people in the university, particularly the faculty." Furthermore, whereas the "outsider" was perceived as less accessible than he actually was, the new president will be perceived as "a man of extraordinary accessibility" even after pressures of the job make accessibility impossible.

The departing president himself professed no sense of alienation from the faculty. Moreover, he did not indicate that he was aware of their alienation from him. He did have educational goals for the institution, many of which involved reorganization but which, he said, were intended ultimately to improve the students' educational experience and to increase faculty members' rewards for good teaching. The constraints on achieving these goals, according to the president, included the limited amount of time he was able to devote to any one objective.

Our evidence about the extent to which the faculty's alienation from this president limited his influence on academic policy is not conclusive. Faculty members claim his impact on them was nil and that, anyway, "department chairpersons are barons at this institution." If the president had had time to propose more programs in the academic realm, he probably would have sensed greater resistance from a faculty convinced he was unsuited by virtue of professional background and administrative style for academic leadership. The contrast between the faculty's reaction to this president and to the preceding and succeeding presidents, however, indicates that the faculty will extend greater emotional support and will be more tolerant of the administrative style of a president with whom they can identify as an academician.

The second case concerns a president from whom faculty members felt quite distant and to whom they were initially hostile; he was not academically acceptable to them and had been "hand-picked by the Regents." This president, however, won their confidence by appointing a provost who, according to the faculty, "was academically a respectable man and who would run the academic side." Faculty members see the education leadership at the institution as "creative interaction" between faculty and provost, and they believe the president is content for it to remain so. Any anxiety the faculty feels about academic policy is focused on the provost, not the president.

This president does not feel removed from academic affairs; he considers himself "responsible for everything that goes on." He is aware that some persons regard his role as external, but he responds that he cannot be effective externally unless he is "deeply aware of what's happening on the campus." He describes himself, however, as a channel for ideas from the inside to the Regents and legislature, and says these ideas usually originate with faculty members, department chairpersons, deans, and provost.

Thus, while this president does not seem to feel that he is restrained from taking a more direct role in education policy, he is content to support others' ideas through his dealings with state officials. Faculty members are confident he is doing a good job and are comfortable with their belief that they and the provost control academic policy: " Faculty members feel that the president's out there fighting for us, the machinery is working, and the senate is doing its job."

The faculty of business and professional schools sometimes identifies with a president from whom the academic faculty feels alienated. One president, because of a nontraditional program he wished to introduce, was seen by the humanities faculty as "a revolutionary, a mover, a shaker who was overturning the old order." At the same time, the professional faculty viewed him as being more in tune with the times than the academic faculty and more responsive to the problems students face in seeking employment.

Likewise, the faculty members of one professional discipline could appreciate a president who did not fit the ideal pattern of educational background and teaching career. They saw in her relationship to the academic faculty parallels to their own relationship to that group:

> She is not an academician in the classical sense of the word, nor am I. I have a doctorate and the president does not, but I'm a social worker. Academics who teach in professional schools tend to be somewhat different from academics who teach in disciplines. She and I are much more alike, for example, in our emphasis on linkages to the community.

This president, perhaps also conscious of the parallel, introduced an interdisciplinary program that would draw on talent from the professional and the arts and sciences faculties. Her intention was partly to cultivate respect among the arts and sciences faculty members for the professional faculty members as intellectuals. The program succeeded both as an educational venture and as a means of alleviating the separation between the academic and the professional faculty (the faculty member's statement quoted above indicates that the sense of difference persists).

Another president, who was a newcomer to the institution and who did not come directly from an academic career, made a decision to establish a professional school without consulting the arts and sciences faculty. In explaining this oversight, he expressed respect for the faculty members; however, he indicated that he looked not to them but to administrators for "initiative." This president has since learned to consult faculty. Some are still resentful, however, and sense an alliance between him and the board of trustees, whom they also perceive as being more responsive to community pressure than to education concerns.

The same president was more successful in initiating a program when he enlisted the help of a senior professor "with a positive attitude toward administration and with the respect of many faculty members" and a committee of faculty and administrators. Some faculty members have reservations about the academic merit of the program, but they see its advantages for the institution and are attempting to make it work. Their response indicates a sensitivity to institutional concerns that presidents tend to underestimate.

Faculty members at several institutions complained that the president seemed hesitant to exert academic leadership. They were especially perplexed at this hesitation when that president had the credentials which would have qualified him or her for that leadership. A president of an institution whose chief executives have traditionally been involved in academic affairs emphasized the necessity of the president's not excluding himself or herself from the academic community. The president must keep informed about who is teaching, what is being taught, and what directions various departments are pursuing; he or she must not let academic policy become the province of deans and provosts. The president cannot "simply come in occasionally to try to exert influence."

Another president described the relationship between the faculty and the president as "a curious love-hate relationship in which faculty members often look for leadership but resent it when it comes." In many instances, they also look for it when it goes.

At the beginning of his administration, a long-term president was directly involved in formulating education policy; he has since become less involved in this endeavor, leaving the faculty with a sense of diminished academic leadership. For the first few years the president taught a class, encouraged all the senior administrators to teach, and chaired two academic policy committees. The hiring of a provost prompted the president to turn over one committee chairmanship. He relinquished the second several years later to avoid a confrontation with the faculty whose union was then pressing to have all committee chairpersons elected. Faculty members now look back nostalgically to the time when he was teaching, when he was his own chief academic officer, and when he could discuss education issues "from other than a budgetary viewpoint."

Faculty members acknowledge the administrative pressures on this president, agree that he is an excellent administrator, and recognize that their desire to elect their own chairpersons nudged him further away from involvement in the educational program. But they also respect most of his educational ideas and miss his leadership: "The president has a way of seeing things very clearly and of expressing his views forcefully and succinctly. I think that if he had been on the curriculum committee and had expressed his views, he might have exercised more leadership than he did."

Contrary to faculty testimony, budgetary concerns have not displaced this president's educational concerns, which he says include such issues as distribution requirements, grade inflation, and faculty involvement in students' personal development. The constraints he notes, besides the pressure to relinquish the committee chairmanships, include the necessity not to "use all his ammunition" by addressing every faculty meeting and not to "overload a committee with administrators," a move that the faculty would resent. This president respected the faculty's prerogatives, and the fact that the faculty members now miss his leadership suggests that they can be too protective of their prerogatives for their own good. At the same time, the president may have overreacted to the committee chairmanship issue.

The Academician-President

One president who was interviewed is reaping the benefits of the faculty's acceptance of him as an academician, but he may be straining that considerable resource. He has a solid academic background as a teacher and administrator at a prestigious university. He was the faculty candidate for his present position, and he continues to teach and publish.

As a relative newcomer to the institution, however, he has "shaken things up" by tightening standards for faculty tenure and by becoming involved in a controversial issue, taking a position opposite to that of the faculty as a whole. A perceptive student body president describes what she calls a serious problem with faculty:

> He's telling them to teach better, advise better, and research better, but not to expect a change in salary, because they're not working hard enough. Then he adds insult to injury with his support of this program because it's a major drain on resources. The faculty members vote and vote and vote to eliminate the program but it seems they're not listened to. The faculty members feel very charmed by him. They believe in him, but his effect is beginning to dwindle a little.

A faculty member notes, however, that because the president is regarded as an academician, the faculty members grant him the benefit of the doubt; they feel that he must be under pressure from the board of trustees, for he would not want to challenge them on this issue.

The easy balance of academic leadership between the faculty and the president at this institution reflects an assumption of mutually compatible values that the insider relationship facilitates. The president believes faculty members are interested in education and in young people and that "it doesn't take much to get them to pursue their own goals in a way that is consonant with the goals defined by the president." A faculty member says the president is "the kind faculty members like to have"—one who "doesn't feel insecure so that he has to associate himself with some kind of educational gimmick." Another adds that educational leadership should come from the departments and that the president's responsibility is to see that it does; this president's style is such that "he can push these things along as pleasantly as possible."

According to the student body president, before this president came "the faculty just didn't give a damn, the administration didn't give a damn, and the students didn't give a damn; when he came, people started thinking about what they wanted from a college." In this case, the president's credentials as a member of the academic community may have given him just the edge he needed to "turn the place around," as a faculty member said, by supporting the faculty's own vision "of what they think the faculty ought to be: good teachers and good scholars."

The case of another academician president confirms the benefits of mutual identification, the relaxation of tension between the president and the faculty on academic policy matters, and improved communication and morale. This president had been in office only a few years when interviewed, but he had been at the institution for many years previously as a faculty member and administrator. He maintains close personal relations with the academic deans and meets regularly with them—so much so that some nonacademic staff members feel slighted—but an administrative colleague considers this close contact natural because the president is "one of them."

The president has used his firm base of personal relations as the central element of his administration. He is "thoroughly resident" and heavily involved in campus life, and he believes this involvement takes him "a long way toward the personal connections that establish faith." It is also a means of self-correction: "You have to be so plugged in to so many people that you feel with them, as a kind of continuing barometer, how things are going and where you're making a mistake." Fellow administrators confirm that their long personal relations with the president have established confidence, given them some "shorthand" in communicating, and allowed them to work out disagreements at an early stage.

The president's intimate knowledge of campus life has been helpful. It has given him an instinct for timing and action that has helped him, for instance, to act in behalf of his constituents during crises when there was no time to assemble the senate.

The president's academic background has established him in students' minds as an educator rather than an administrator: he was "an educator for a long time before he became an administrator and he hasn't lost those qualities." The students credit him with being very involved in academic policy, specifically with protecting academic freedom at their institution.

Administrators, too, see him as "first of all an academician" who "went into the presidency and administration with mixed emotions." An associate says, in fact, that the president could afford to be more forceful about his educational goals because the faculty members "respect him as an academic." A faculty member suggests, however, that the president's relationship with the faculty is a nonthreatening one that a presumption of academic leadership might upset. Educational direction comes from the faculty through the academic senate rather than from either the president or provost, and the president supports faculty preeminence in academic policy. The president himself feels that his role is to create conditions in which constituents can "spawn, develop, create, and innovate" programs.

Other presidents whom the academic community tolerated less easily seemed more determined to achieve particular programs. That this president, a firmly established member of the academic community, would defer to the faculty on academic policy perhaps seems paradoxical. But this president identifies so closely with faculty members as a group that he sees little distinction between their educational values and his own. In this case, the balance seems to be working well, with most constituents satisfied that educational leadership is emanating from a trustworthy source.

An Optimal Case

An institution benefits from having a president who is accepted by and feels himself or herself to be a member of the academic community. One such president was a long-time faculty member and department chairman in the faculty of arts and sciences at the college before becoming its president, and he continues to teach. During the first year of his presidency, some faculty members felt they had to remind him he was "no longer a member of the faculty." Now, however, they see him as "not separate from the faculty but part of it" and own him an intellectual as well as an institutional leader.

As in the case described earlier, long-term relationships have contributed to mutual trust and easy communication. As a result, many of the president's colleagues are not afraid to argue with him; thus, they are a particularly valuable resource for this president, whom some constituents hold in awe. Moreover, his acceptance by and respect for the faculty have helped him achieve solutions to some of the college's problems, both administrative and educational.

Referring to the president's inaugural statement in which he announced some innovative intentions, a faculty member said the president "did not display a clear sensitivity to what was and *wasn't* possible." But, in fact, one of his strengths is that he has not lost his sense of what *is* possible. (It was said of another president in the study that she "knew people's faults too well" and therefore "knew what *wasn't* possible.") Part of this president's belief in possibility comes from his retaining his identification with the faculty.

The president enlisted faculty members to design and develop his innovative projects. He is realistic about the "slow and cumbersome" faculty decision-making process, but he feels that he should allow time for it to work rather than to try to impose solutions on the faculty. It took three years, for instance, to implement a new academic program the president proposed, but the faculty is strongly behind it. No one has said of this president (as was said of others) that he despairs of accomplishing anything through the faculty senate "because of the Mickey Mouse that goes on there."

A feature of this administration is the president's belief in sharing with faculty members and other constituents information that had previously been considered confidential. One president who was interviewed acknowledged that he felt faculty members had nothing to contribute to discussions of practical matters and, thus, had not consulted them. This president, in contrast, has established two advisory councils on important areas of administrative policy; the councils are composed of representatives of all constituencies, including members from the different faculties. One motivation for such openness is his identification with faculty members: "When I was a member of this faculty, one of our constant complaints was that key decisions seemed to be made in secret. I have not heard any such complaints since the new councils have been in existence."

When he was a faculty member at the college, this president gained valuable knowledge of the institution's problems, and this knowledge has led him to seek solutions to these problems. As a department chairman, he learned, for instance, that there was no system that would check a department's rate of spending or warn the chairperson when the department's financial commitments were over budget; therefore, he introduced a new budget system. Many presidents spoke of the problems caused by departmentalism, but this president was one of the few to acknowledge it is not limited to the faculty: "All departments—whether academic or administrative—protect their own turf."

Another factor working in this president's favor is that he identifies with his constituents' lack of understanding of the president's job. As a result, he is not bitter about that lack of understanding.

> It took me some years to learn that no constituency really understands the full range of the president's responsibilities. I am certainly no exception. I had been here many years before I became president, and I was very interested in general college affairs, but I was totally amazed at the wide variety of tasks I had to do as president that I did not anticipate.

He works especially hard at communicating with students, "the constituency that least understands the presidency." (Their testimony indicates otherwise.) Although at first he worried least about the faculty, who had known him for a long time, he later realized that many new faculty members had never even seen him except from a distance, and he took measures to meet with them.

The president-faculty relationship, says a faculty member, is not adversarial; the president has little faculty opposition, and there is no talk of unionization. The fact that the president came from faculty ranks helps him, and he has increased faculty members' respect for him by demonstrating his intelligence, rationality, and administrative ability. He has also been politically wise in his dealings with them. They appreciate the fact that he hasn't taken resources from them to help the financially pressed professional schools. Moreover, a change to year-round operation has permitted an increase in the size of the faculty. Thus, faculty members have a sense of security not enjoyed by their colleagues at many institutions. On a rare occasion when the faculty did challenge him, the president's faith in open communication helped restore peace.

> I think I have a reputation for telling the faculty the truth, and that reputation has made the difference. The meeting was billed as a bloody faculty meeting, and it didn't turn out to be anything of the sort. I took the initiative to raise the issue—telling them all the

details and what the decisions were and why they were made—
and then gave them a chance to ask me any question they wished
in public. In this way, the issue became completely diffused.

He repeatedly demonstrates that he believes in the rationality and
good sense of his constituents and expects them to recognize these
qualities in himself.

A president referred to earlier acquired the image of a corporation
executive because of efficiency measures he took. This president, in
contrast, has avoided that image, according to a faculty member, even
though he was involved in implementing a new management information system: "The faculty members do not perceive the president's
role in implementing the system as a new management procedure but
as him tinkering at the terminal. That image has a personal element,
and the faculty members do not get upset that they've been 'manager-
ized' into a new system."

This president has full credentials for being accepted by the
academic community, and he has worked at maintaining their acceptance. But the quality that makes him a true member of the community
is that he feels himself to be one. He remembers what it was like to be
a faculty member. He does not analyze "the academic mind" as
though it were alien to him; he does not describe faculty deliberations
in derisive terms; he does not despair of involving faculty members in
issues broader than their academic disciplines. As president, he enjoys
being able to solve institutional problems that as a faculty member he
could only recognize, but he is proud to be called "professor": "As a
teacher, you have a quite different relationship with the students. It's
an unwritten rule that they never call me 'President' in the classroom;
it's always 'Professor.' This may seem like a small point, but believe
me, it is not."

This president, who has been described as nearly ideal, does not
owe his outstanding administration solely to his close identification
with faculty members. He is a brilliant scholar and thus has credibility
among other scholars. Moreover, he demonstrates considerable administrative talent inasmuch as he has been able to identify and
address the institution's major problems. But his relationship to the
faculty, developed over many years as an academic colleague, has
been a crucial factor in his success. Few presidents have had such a
foundation for their administration.

The ideal relationship between a president and the faculty should
be one of mutual respect and acceptance. In terms of the well-being of
a college or university—for example, institutional morale and prob-

lem solving—it is perhaps more important that the president closely identifies with faculty members than that faculty members identify with the president. A president from whom faculty members feel alienated will encounter more resistance to his or her ideas on education policy, more suspicion of motives, and less tolerance of managerial and external activities than one whom they see as an academician like themselves. Most presidents, nevertheless, are able to affect educational policy if they try.

Nonacademician or nontraditional presidents, despite the handicaps of being held at bay and judged more critically than other presidents, have made significant contributions to their institutions, particularly in the areas of interdisciplinary and community outreach programs. These innovations have been most successful when the president has had enough confidence in the faculty members to be candid with them about his or her objectives and to invite them to participate in the planning and implementation of the new programs. Even faculty members who resented what they saw as an intrusion into their territory said they were glad that their president's nontraditional approach had helped the institution financially—in one case probably making the difference between its survival and closure.

Faculty morale can remain high at institutions where faculty members feel distant from the president but closely allied to a chief academic officer whom they consider "academically respectable." Conversely, when a president acceptable to the academic community remains aloof from education policy, faculty members may resent what they see as a lack of leadership, especially if there is no strong academic officer to take up the slack.

The Presidency Project's sample indicates that faculty morale is highest when the president has proper academic credentials and an acceptable style, shows an interest in academic policy and faculty projects, and does not seem to impose his or her ideas or overstep his or her authority. Such a president has a good opportunity to participate with the faculty in formulating educational policy. If the president also sees himself or herself as a member of the academic community, the probability is enhanced that he or she will engage the faculty in working out solutions to the institution's problems. As someone who identifies with faculty members, the president knows their concerns, respects their decision-making authority and processes, values their ideas and seriously considers their objections to his or her own ideas. More important, such a president will see their values and goals as compatible to his or her own—able to be broadened or raised but not circumvented.

4 Presidents in Action: The Executive, the Person

The Mystique of the Presidency

A university president once summed up the satisfactions that the job afforded him: "One of my greatest pleasures has been getting to know these people and learning at least a little bit about their interests and their work. For me, the real enjoyment of the job comes from personal associations with a remarkable array of lively and interesting and good people."[1]

That statement happened to be made during an early morning interview. The president of another institution had this to say at a later hour in the day: "Some days I feel as if I've been a punching bag all day. I come home sick and tired of being the symbol of authority for all these kids who are trying to find out how to deal with authority."

A third president, meanwhile, reported in writing to his university community:

> A university such as ours—labor-intensive, heavily dependent on enrollment for its income, a heavy user of fuel oil, electric power, and telephone service, and with a payroll that is 66 percent of its total budget—is fearfully vulnerable to the threat of reduced income and an inflationary economy. All demographic analysts point to a declining population of high school graduates, and there is no assurance that double-digit increases in the cost of living are behind us. The future holds little that is bright or comfortable.

And from the president of one of the four largest campuses in the United States:

> There's always a hassle of some kind—a letter from the Office on Civil Rights challenging the affirmative action program, for example, and you're in a shouting match with the regulatory bodies. You're stereotyped in a variety of ways by your critics. The blacks stereotype you as antiblack; the activist women stereotype you as antiwoman, and so forth.

In his study *Presidential Search* (1979), John Nason reported findings from more than 300 presidential search procedures annually

1. *University: A Princeton Quarterly*, Summer 1976, no. 69, p. 19.

conducted by boards of trustees throughout the country. Even before state and federal passage of so-called sunshine legislation, most institutions customarily compiled lists of 100 to 150 candidates. In 1948, Antioch selected Douglas MacGregor from some 665 prospects; he stayed in office only three and a half years and then returned to research and writing on human relationships in social organizations. The institution then had to repeat the search process. Today the lists of candidates, including self-nominees, often contain more than 200 names.

Who wants to be a college president? Evidently a great many people. Despite the adversities of declining enrollment, increasing deficits, and program cutbacks, the prospect lists still stretch out before search committees like Jacob Marley's chain. These lists continue to grow until a deadline is imposed.

Do the persons eventually selected as president stay in office for a shorter period of time today? Statistics show they do not. Since World War II, various studies have attempted to measure the average length of a president's term of office. These studies must make several determinations, such as whether to count the terms of acting presidents and when to start counting tenure—from the time a president takes office or from the time of official inauguration, which may occur as late as a year after the president has taken office. Each study analyzes the data differently.

Most of the findings, however, tend to parallel closely William Selden's findings in 1960: the average length of a president's term is five to seven years.[2] If an institution is experiencing hard times, the president tends to stay in office longer. During such times, an institution tends to blame reverses on external problems and to rally behind the executive who is trying to cope with them.

Of the twenty-five presidents who were interviewed for the Presidency Project, eight have left office. Three have assumed other presidencies, one has taken a senior academic administrative post, and three have begun or resumed careers outside academe. At this writing, three of the seventeen presidents still in office have announced their resignation. One will return to teaching, and two have not revealed career plans. All but one of the presidents left office by choice and at a time of their own choosing. The length of their term of office ranged from five to twenty-one years.

2. William Selden, "How Long Is a College President?" *AAC Bulletin* (Washington, D.C.: Association of American Colleges, 1960).

None of the presidents interviewed said he or she regretted the choice of career, although all freely discussed its rough spots. Other persons interviewed at the same institutions, however, voiced much criticism of the president. Most of the criticism concerned faults of omission rather than faults of commission. No one flatly stated that the president's election had been a mistake or that the campus had suffered as a result of it. Several persons interviewed were critical of outright displays of executive power, such as the failure to consult with constituents or other administrators before taking central action, the tendency to let other administrators announce bad news, and so forth. Other persons approved of the president's use of authority and admired his willingness to make a decision and face the heat. One person expressed this approval thus: "He has the guts to fire people when they need to be fired."

Staff members who had borne the brunt of unilateral administrative action directly charged the president with full-blown autocracy. During this century, autocratic presidents have in the main been found only at small, often parochial institutions under sectarian control. If they occasionally are found at more sophisticated institutions, they almost always initiate controversy that reaches beyond the campus, and because they are such rare birds on the college scene, they inevitably get much publicity. The fact that trustees sometimes rally behind such presidents reveals the continuing gaps between lay and academic beliefs about how college education ought to be directed; it does not necessarily indicate that such occurrences are frequent or that most presidents lust for power. The presidents of large universities, of course, cannot avoid autocracy when crucial decisions must be made quickly.

The Presidency Project did not bring to light any presidential longing, wistful or otherwise, for autocratic rule. College and university presidents do possess power, but few presidents seek the office simply for the sake of power. We sought to resolve two questions: (1) What do college and university presidents most desire to accomplish with their power? and (2) What are the constraints on their use of this power?

Readers of the history of higher education may be inclined to dwell on the builder presidents, who dominated American university growth from the 1860s until the 1930s. W. H. Cowley, one of the most knowledgeable historians of higher education, portrayed these builders as titans in his book *Presidents, Professors, and Trustees: The*

Evolution of American Academic Government (1980). Cowley refers to the period 1870–1910 as the "age of titans" and illustrates the breed with Andrew White, of Cornell University, James B. Angell, of the University of Michigan, C. W. Eliot, of Harvard University, Joseph Gilman, of Johns Hopkins University, and William Rainey Harper, of the University of Chicago. Many other institutions of lesser national prominence were also transformed by builder presidents, many of whom had stepped into the role from high positions in the hierarchy of the institution's sponsoring church.

In the early twentieth century, college and university organization underwent two major changes. First, presidents found that the challenge of presiding called for full-time administrative effort. They broke with the tutelary model in which the president might teach from one to four classes, typically including a course in moral philosophy. Second, college and university administration was diversified to include other full-time officers. In the early 1900s, "the staff" originally consisted only of the dean of the college, but by midcentury it had become a full complement of special officers now accepted as part of the equipage of collegiate organization.

Today's president thus inherits a structure that mandates a management role. To the professoriate, however, the word *manager* connotes an administrator who has waived his or her right to collegiality; the only term more distasteful than *manager* is *boss*. Yet at least four developments since 1960 have expanded the president's managerial role. First, the range of high school graduates who attend college has broadened considerably; many students with limited academic ability now go on to college. Second, the drop in the number of 18–24-year-olds has resulted in the decrease in potential college enrollees, a decrease that will continue until the mid-1990s. Third, the grim enrollment outlook and other threats to faculty members' self-interests have led to an increase in the faculty's sense of job insecurity and, thus, an increase in unionization. Fourth, financial pressures are increasing on all sides. These pressures are fueled by inflation, reduced appropriations, and the increasingly commercial mentality of students today who reject the long-range vocational approach of liberal education, an attitude apparent even among G.I. students after World War II.

Because of these developments, a president who believes that learning is an adventure finds it more and more difficult to see a clear path from the managerial responsibilities of the office to the personal leadership that adventure requires. To have the opportunity for this personal leadership, someone interested in learning should aim for the top spot in academic administration per se: the position of vice president for academic affairs, vice president and dean of faculty, or provost (at some medium-sized colleges as well as at large universities, the provost is considered second in command, essentially the inside president, responsible for "educational affairs" in the largest sense).[3]

Has the contemporary college or university president become the executive manager as well as chief public relations officer, with responsibilities in the field equal to those on campus? Is it necessary or even appropriate today for the president to be a professional educator? Need he or she continue to be a spokesperson for education policy, much less propose it, refine it, and shepherd it through the legislative process until it is approved by the faculty and the board?

The presidents interviewed consistently responded that they think about their leadership role a great deal, even as they go about their managerial day. The interviews also revealed that, popular opinion to the contrary, other persons on campus also think about the president's role. Although faculty members and students hold hard to the right to campus freedoms and participation in policy decisions affecting them, they also want a president who is a president in the positive sense of the word. Such expectations, of course, can easily become inflated. The most common reply to the question of what the president ideally should be and do was, "Well, after all, the job's an impossible one." But the next remark just as commonly was, "He (or she) ought to change such and such."

Approaching the Realities of the President's Campus Function

The Presidency Project focused on the chief executive as a person dealing simultaneously with traditional functions and with the contemporary realities of the American college or university. Spending fifty hours talking privately with college presidents about themselves is an experience that faculty members might rank as sufficiently horrible to have been included in Dante's *Inferno*. But this experience reinforced the notion that a college or university's administration is influenced by its particular setting and by the times.

As noted earlier, a president's perspective on even the most general topic of education is often affected by the length of his or her term of office. Other variables that affected these presidents' views

---

3. In *multiversities*, a term traced not to Clark Kerr, as commonly thought, but to the late Whitney Oates of Princeton, an executive vice president may supersede the provost or replace that office.

were related to the date of our interview: the institution's position vis-à-vis the annual budget cycle; the institution's position vis-à-vis the faculty tenure cycle; the length of time before or since a governing board meeting; and the latest campus issue, especially if it were an issue discussed in the public press. To professional critics of technique, such variables of time and circumstance may discredit the validity of the project's open approach so far as administrative analysis is concerned. We would argue, however, that most questionnaires, which most presidents pull from the mail pile at the end of a working day and answer by rapidly punching out computer card holes, do not yield more thoughtful or valid answers.

The most important question in our interviews concerned the presidents' own priorities for the future. The presidents were asked to describe how they were accustomed to working with fellow administrators, faculty members, and students in order to pursue these priorities. The questions covered procedures and styles of dealing with faculty members, students, and the customary cabinet of second-line officers, typically vice presidents (except in the smallest schools).

Also of great interest to the Presidency Project was the position the faculty members and students accorded the president in the area of education leadership. The variety of academic officers' titles indicates more than the lack of pattern in the taxonomy of public administration. Discussions of campus titles led to discussions about where the president stood at that college as a leader in education. We wanted to learn what role the president plays in such areas as curriculum policy, program innovation, faculty appointments, promotion or retention, and, most important, the setting of institutional goals. In most cases, the responses made clear that these topics are of recurrent interest on campus. The differences of opinion about the leader's role reinforce the notion that the president's power derives from the open-endedness of his or her assignment.

Certain of the responses will be related in detail for two reasons. First, they provide a base on which campus appraisal of the president is weighed. Second and more important, the responses indicate the degree of education leadership that American college and university presidents as a group are providing. Current speculation is that the president's influence as a leader in education in all but small, traditional institutions is almost nil.

Despite the variety of institutions, administrative structures, and prevailing local circumstances, most of the presidents interviewed, regardless of institution, seem to be facing similar problems and experiencing similar results. The data derived from the interviews typically reflect the ups and downs of a president's activities—feelings of frustration or stalemate, or the glimmer of a breakthrough at the end of each day.

Whether the institution was a small college or a huge university, the same key problems came to the surface. Regardless of the size of the budget or the endowment, "people problems" prevailed. These problems concerned the adequacy of resources for various projects; strategies for winning support for ideas for change from faculty members, students, and outside constituents; consideration of constituents' wishes, most of which, given the financial climate of the times, must be postponed or turned down; and the settling of disagreements or the response to malcontents.

Throughout their interviews, the presidents focused on the uses of presidential power in the face of issues that continuously confront them. As preceding chapters illustrate, the college and university president retains considerable power, a power perhaps as well supported and as little curbed by statute as that in any modern social organization.

Presidential Polarities: Preserving the Institution versus Leading the Institution

The attitudes of the presidents interviewed ranged from selfless dedication to candid interest in self-advancement. This range of viewpoints was reflected by the staff members interviewed as well as by the presidents. As recorded by the interviews, two presidential priorities recurred: the institution's integrity in the sense of literally holding itself together; and the president's assurance of his personal concern for each individual within that institution. These priorities will serve as guidelines for a closer examination of what the chief executive wants most to accomplish, what procedures and styles are employed toward those ends, and how these matters are interpreted by other administrators, by faculty leaders, and by students who have continuing personal contact with the president.

The necessity of holding the institution together was implicit in the conversations with each president. If the institution was in financial straits, the word *survival* was freely used. *Survival* also entered into discussions at institutions whose balance sheets might be the envy of most other colleges and universities. One of the universities in our sample receives the largest amount of federal research and training grant moneys awarded to any institution in the United States. To its president, *survival* means maintaining that high level of government support; any loss of this funding will bring lamentations from constituents, if not the departure of key persons from the institution.

For most of the presidents, personal concerns about the status of faculty members, students, and staff members were equally important as the task of holding the institution together financially. Executives who seemed to communicate well with their constituents were less inclined to be referred to as "a manager" if not immediately given the accolade, "He (or she) is a leader." A modern college or university, whether large or small, must be well managed. Some faculty members wonder whether good management should be the sum of the president's virtues. One faculty member, expressing delight over the new university president and his rich academic background, climaxed his point with the comment, "He doesn't act like a manager." Another faculty member, almost incredulous, said of his president, "He isn't an administrator; he's an educator."

The necessity of raising funds, balancing budgets by trimming programs, and controlling raging utility costs has long since relieved presidents of the need to apologize for using the term *management* to describe their principal occupation. (The term is still used sparingly in front of academic colleagues.) When faculty members first began unionizing, the presiding officer across the bargaining table could only be identified as representing management. In earlier days, the term *manager* posed no difficulties for renowned university heads such as Samuel P. Capen, who wrote *The Management of Universities* (1953). Even purists can relax: for decades one widely accepted definition of the administration of education has been "the management of change." No president can escape the responsibility of that mandate, although some have tried.

If management is the inescapable leading requirement of the head of a social organization, why should it affect judgments of presidential leadership? Why can it not be a means of appraising effectiveness in carrying out the purposes of the office? For the governing board as well as for many on campus whose lives are affected by the manner in which the institution is run, the president's skills in managing the multiple responsibilities of the office are the main elements in evaluating performance.

Resistance to the term *manager* derives from an attitude as deep in the scholar as it is in the artist or the inventor: none of these persons wants to be managed any more than he or she wishes to be known as an employee. Amitai Etzioni, in *A Comparative Analysis of Complex*

Organizations (1961), categorizes as R (rank) organizations those enterprises staffed by highly educated, individualized people who plan their own working days. These he distinguishes from L (line) organizations (e.g., the military) and T (top) organizations, the latter best represented by outright executive autocracy (a few examples can still be found in American colleges and universities here and there).

The head of an R organization has an especially sensitive assignment if, in addition to carrying out the necessities of management, he or she wishes to lead by establishing a "leader-follower mutuality of goals," a concept that James MacGregor Burns has set forth in *Leadership* (1978). This style imposes a special kind of self-restraint: the president must induce the faculty's acceptance of his or her leadership by setting an example of that leadership—for example, by proposing, but not dictating, a new program. Moreover, management decisions themselves should be approached through consultation and a readiness to heed the results of such consultation when feasible.

Such self-restraint may simply not be feasible, however, when megamillion budget deadlines and central-system due dates are on the president's desk. The more complex the institution, the fewer examples of creative leadership as described by Burns were revealed in the interviews.

President G., head of one of the smaller institutions in our sample, admitted to having changed his mind on a decision after consultation with a faculty council. His comments about style were likewise revealing: "I try to get to know as many of the faculty members as possible." He listed among his top priorities the restoration of collegiality and the faculty members' faith in administrators as persons willing to compromise and not over-eager to impose decisions. A faculty member at that same campus confirmed the democratic trend: one of the president's top priorities is "to reinstall the faculty in education policy making."

Does this approach indicate leadership or the abandonment of leadership? One test can be the relationship between the president and the chief academic officer. A vice provost gave credit to President G. for respecting the faculty members and giving them a greater sense of responsibility. The president himself commented that in consultations he operates with "a pad of paper for my brain." Still, neither faculty members nor students voiced any criticism of indecisiveness on the president's part when important issues had to be faced. A group of student leaders put it plainly: "He's a nice person, and we believe in him." They reserved their discontent for the state education system and the state's reactionary governor. This university president apparently became a successful leader in education by developing leadership in his subordinates. His example has perhaps been lost to history by the inhospitality of the state setting. Since this interview, he has left office to assume the presidency of a small private college in the West.

To manage and manage well, no matter how large the institution, is the inescapable responsibility of the college or university president. The question remains whether contemporary college and university heads do anything besides manage. Are they able, in one way or another, personally to fulfill the role of educator, or do they delegate this responsibility to the senior academic officer? Our sample indicates that most presidents favor delegation.

Alternatives such as the question of delegation versus personal action offer little help unless some criteria can be established for the educator president, a symbol found in the writings of Robert Hutchins, Harold Dodds, and Kingman Brewster. (Presumably, these presidents could be spared from their managerial responsibilities long enough at least to *write* about the problems of educators.) Some renowned presidents continue to make headlines on national political and social issues. Yet when their own operations are examined, they show themselves to be institutional managers with enough charisma and display of decision making to convince their campus constituency that their influence on the education process is personal and direct. To some persons on campus, particularly to senior faculty members, the president is not considered to be an educator but the executive and facilitator of others who are educators. Any published responses to questionnaires about the college or university presidency will reflect this stance.

The type of president most likely to win honors as an educator may be the university president so widely regarded that almost anything he or she says becomes newsworthy. The presidents of some large universities work hard at creating a public life that extends beyond their institutional job. Most presidents in our sample, including the president of an institution with forty campus branches and a budget of nearly a half billion, feel that they have sufficiently fulfilled their responsibilities as president if the institution is supplied and managed well enough to fulfill its multiple missions of research, teaching, and public service.

Another manager president in line for recognition as a force in education is the executive who by sheer drive and tireless appearances on and off campus picks up a college on its way down and brings to it new resources, increased enrollment, and regional attention. Yet the techniques used in this case are more likely to be those of the take-charge, all-purpose manager than those of the leader of intellectuals.

President B., who among those interviewed best exemplified the take-charge approach, was candid enough to state that he opposed some major positions recently taken by the faculty and that some of his own ideas about education had stirred faculty opposition. "If the faculty members are united behind an idea," he said, "I don't oppose them." His efforts to publicize the college have brought the institution better financial health and regional support. To use James MacGregor Burns's terms once more, this president has furnished *transactional* rather than *transforming* leadership; that is, he has worked for agreements and reciprocal advantages, leaving the character and educational mission of the institution essentially unchanged. To lead in ways that impel genuine change of ideas or programs or, hardest of all, basic purpose—in other words, to transform an institution by inspiring willing followers who then lead the institution toward these changes—is a rare accomplishment. Five of the twenty-five presidents interviewed evidenced a capacity for transforming leadership. Their leadership will be discussed at the end of this chapter.

A president who desires to be a leader in education must reconcile that desire with the necessity of being a manager. During our interviews, it became progressively clear that education leadership and management are no longer considered mutually exclusive tasks. Higher education history is full of stories of presidents who, because they found management either too distasteful or too tough to deal with, held office only briefly. Because the Presidency Project focused on clarifying purpose and attitude rather than making appraisals of institutions, the interviewers acknowledged the necessity of the president's role as a manager. What remained to be explored was how or whether presidents can be leaders in education as well as managers of the process of educating. Toward what ends do they lead? By what procedures and through what styles? And in what ways does their leadership set them apart from the management of any other organization?

Presidential Leadership Styles

What follows is a series of categories of presidential styles that were observed to characterize institutional leadership. In each case, the style was linked with examples of others so that a classification of presidential behavior in office might be collated from our sample of twenty-five.

The Take-Charge President

Holding together an institution—whatever its size, structure, or current problems—is a heavy burden. An institution suffering through difficulties—for example, the effects of a preceding administration that simply slumbered—cries out for an executive with the character and energy to confront these problems in a highly visible way.

Six of the presidents—that is, less than one-fourth of those interviewed—impressed us as take-charge persons. Each exhibited certain qualities that no doubt helped ensure that their term of service was long and effective: solid experience, a steady manner, moderate views on education issues, and a willingness to make personal decisions without impetuosity or hesitance.

The first of these take-charge presidents, President B., had taken over a slumping denominational college and reinvigorated it with a vitality that became well publicized. He remains closely identified with the college's public image although his distance from faculty thinking is not considered to be one of his strong features.

President R., the second take-charge executive in this category, was for twenty years president of a well-regarded college of liberal arts. He has since retired. He moved fairly well with the general trends toward faculty participation in governance without losing his reputation as a person who, to quote a faculty member, "can dig in his heels and bring you full circle back to his point."

President R. is said to have covered the campus widely, to have willingly shared his time and his turf, and to have had a "prodigious" memory. For many years, he chaired the curriculum committee. A senior professor observed, "He is becoming less of an education leader and more of a businessman." He could keep on top of controversial issues and would do extra homework before a critical committee session. His campus was relatively calm during the turbulent sixties; his presidency was never seriously challenged. He was "enormously popular with the board." The faculty acknowledged that he was the boss, even something of a father figure. His personality to some who had known him for a long time, however, remained hard to fathom. For example, when he retired there was uncertainty about what the farewell gift should be.

According to the students interviewed, President R. presided with force and integrity. They complimented his management skill, yet a former foreign language teacher called him "essentially an academi-cian." The students regretted that he was so busy that he had not had time to influence personally the student community. The possibility that his power might intimidate rather than stimulate a student's growth was the only unfavorable comment recorded.

This take-charge president thus retired as a sturdy man who had been ensconced in a region reflecting his own nature and nurture. Did he attempt to change the college's approach to education during twenty years in office? It may be significant that he did not deal with that question during the interview, nor could the interviewer have asked it without introducing a directive note that was not emerging by itself. Identification and a sense of constancy adhered to this adminis-tration; that fact emerged from the interviews with others, and was obviously reassuring to some. Younger staff members, it is true, were more inclined to confess a readiness for change.

Two of the other six take-charge presidents bear analysis because both preside over huge institutions yet have different management styles. President O., who manages a very large university and also oversees its several dozen branches throughout the state, has a highly visible management style. His organization is an example of fairly orthodox Weberian bureaucracy with layers of well-defined and distributed responsibilities. He relies on a strong provost, the acknowl-edged second in command, to coordinate academic policy. Regarding his own role as an educator, he commented, "I would guess that the faculty sees me as someone who got this thing [i.e., this large sprawl-ing megaversity] started, and that at least now we have an academic officer who is in charge of the academic process." Still the president was "the boss" to everyone else interviewed. A usually cheerful person, he likes to be liked and will, on occasion, drop in on student social functions.

The head of the second large institution, President M., unlike President O., worked his way up through the lines of academic administration. President M. spends much time in academic councils and committees, more often than not as chairperson. He sees his role as setting the education goals for his university. His approach is to draw up his own statements of education goals, distribute these to faculty and administrative policy groups for review and suggested revisions, and then submit them to the board of trustees for approval as part of the university's mission.

To the puzzlement of colleagues, President M. has never desig-nated a second in command among the six vice presidents, nor is the academic affairs vice president considered the first among equals.

The president is a stickler for doing homework so that he can be as familiar with detailed matters as are his subordinates. He is relaxed with students and accessible to them. At the same time, the general opinion is that once he makes up his mind about a matter, he seldom changes it, even if students petition him to change.

Students see President M. as "essentially a manager," yet emphasize his evident desire to manage everything that is considered important to the university's welfare as an educational institution. A senior professor summed up the administration with a rare compliment: "I think he's doing a reasonable job." Still those faculty members interviewed warned explicitly that President M. should not become involved in the issue of what should be taught or how. At this university, as at other institutions with a well-established faculty, judicial and executive powers are acknowledged to be presidential territory, but academic initiative is considered off limits to the president. Yet at almost every campus, faculty members said that they wanted "a president with vision."

The final two executives exemplify other traits common to take-charge presidents. The first, President E., moved from the presidency of the medical college of a neighboring university to the presidency of a large and complex institution, which he reorganized considerably in six years. His medical background and his large impressive stature were balanced by an evident desire to operate by competence and decisiveness rather than charisma. A fellow administrator comments: "He might have worked harder at making personal contact with the faculty members. If he had made some slight changes of style, other constituencies might have been a little softer on him."

The interviewer, who knew President E. personally, feels that he may have had more potential for leadership than was shown during his term in office. The take-charge person often does not open up enough of himself or herself to inspire the active followership that James MacGregor Burns believes to be an essential element in leadership: "The role of the 'great man' need not be diminished. . . . That role is all the more legitimate . . . if top leaders help make their followers into leaders."[4]

The sixth take-charge president, President K., came to office under unusual circumstances. First, he assumed the presidency immediately after a college controversy embroiling the board chairman and the then-president, who was ultimately discharged. Second,

4. James MacGregor Burns, *Leadership* (New York: Harper and Row, 1978), p. 443.

he came into office from a nonacademic profession. The circumstances were not related, but each may have influenced President K.'s motives, for he served as president for many years and was generally acknowledged to be a strong person in office.

A lengthy interview with President K. brought out his view that liberal education sees the world as its classroom. As a result, he has made a "very strong effort to see to it that every administrator of every rank perceived himself or herself—and was perceived by the faculty—as an educator." A college faculty could not be expected to adopt this view enthusiastically. As a senior professor remarked, one effect has been to weaken the identity of just who and what the faculty is.

President K. has used his influence to build up campus activities in the college student center—such as band, photography, film making, and crafts—with teachers who operate on a noncredit basis. He is against the "cocurricular approach" and has not moved to change a conventional academic curriculum. When the faculty delays in resolving an issue, he makes the decision. In addition, control of appointments and tenure remains in administrative hands. President K. tolerates open disagreement in faculty meetings, although he reportedly becomes defensive if he is not aware of such disagreements in advance.

Our impression of this take-charge administration is somewhat like that of President B., cited at the outset of this series. President K. concedes that the plenary faculty should decide the formal course of study. He has also managed to use his influence in loosening certain academic standards. The college now competes with colleges of established prestige. And President K., following a cardinal rule of the take-charge president, gives unremitting attention to every issue that could conceivably affect the college's reputation both on and off campus.

Students perceive this dedication and regard it as the mark of an effective college manager. They wish he could spend more time on campus, however. One student remarked, "I wish that students at some point could just sit down with him, like we're sitting with you now, and talk."

The Standard-Bearer President

For seven of the twenty-five presidents interviewed for the Presidency Project, the term *standard-bearer* seems to be most appropriate. The term refers to the status of the institution over which these presidents preside, namely, the state of "having arrived." This state depends on a number of factors, one of which is environment. How an institution is judged depends considerably on the status of other institutions in its region. In some areas, the happy condition of being considered "to have arrived" may reflect a scarcity of nearby competition. In others, it points to a geographic region where well-regarded colleges and universities have existed for many decades, such as the Connecticut River valley or the Nashville, Tennessee, area. Other factors that affect the state of a standard-bearer institution are its enrollment curve, its annual operating statement, and its balance sheet. Most standard-bearer institutions offer a conventional curriculum that centers on the liberal arts or the basic sciences and engineering.

In the past dozen years, financial realities have affected even standard-bearer institutions. Otherwise sound colleges and universities, those thought to "have it made" (the expression must be considered relative in higher education economics, even at Harvard) have discovered that the stratified nature of student demand can cause anxiety and can force them to compete with other institutions for resources and clientele. Minter and Bowen, in their fourth annual financial survey of. 100 sample schools *(Private Higher Education, 1978)*, discovered that the liberal arts level II institutions, which generally receive fewer funds than liberal arts level I institutions and doctorate-granting universities, were showing persistent signs of fiscal strain to a greater extent than in previous years.[5]

On the other hand, standard-bearer institutions are found among both the liberal arts level I institutions and doctorate-granting universities. By no means do all of them enjoy the inelastic student market (rising applications accompanied by rising tuition) that would justify their being classed as elite. In the United Sates, there are no more than fifty "elite" institutions, most of them private. At most of these institutions, the president does not have to think about the budget every hour of the day, although no president admits to having an easy mind on the point, not even presidents of leading state universities with their huge operating appropriations and billion-dollar physical plants. As has already been noted, the meaning of *survival* varies according to the commitments that the institution has already made.

Presidents of standard-bearer institutions were asked this pertinent question: Where is this institution headed and how much can you

5. These college classifications were furnished by the Carnegie Council's *A Classification of Institutions of Higher Education,* 1976.

as president do to lead it in that direction? The question proved to be a challenging one. If solvency, not to mention a modest surplus, is reasonably assured, a certain acceptance in the educational world may be assumed. Academic excellence—the term by now shows signs of semantic exhaustion—is taken as established (granted, there is always room for improvement). Institutionwide moves into new or experimental curricula are rare among standard-bearer colleges and universities. As keepers of a regional standard of esteem, they typically change slowly and then only along conventional lines.

Data from the interviews reveal three patterns of movement among the standard-bearer presidents. Three of the presidents were concerned with strengthening their institution's base. Two of them presided over women's colleges that for years have had solid academic reputations but that now need more resources and a more widely publicized record of accomplishment; the standards could slip if competition continues to grow. New programs, more emphasis on career options, and more vigorous alumni and parent involvement have all been features of the efforts to strengthen the institutional base.

The third president concerned with strengthening the institution's base had recently accepted the presidency of a prestigious private university that had suffered serious financial reverses and was in danger of losing programs and status. His vigorous, comprehensive leadership style could almost categorize him as a take-charge president. The difference is that this president, who had recently come from a university with an exceptionally strong faculty, adheres to procedures of shared governance and genuine consultation. He also has maintained collegiality through such actions as teaching a course in his field (Southern history).

Two of the standard-bearer presidents feel that their institution's present position is secure (dollar and enrollment statistics would justify their contentment). In fact, these two presidents have been such effective managers that they have improved the financial position and the prestige of their institution. One has served for five years, the other for ten.

These two presidents are now asking, What's next? One described his remaining goals candidly: he would like to see his college one rung higher on the ladder of prestige in its region, a region that encompasses three of the acknowledged elite coed liberal arts colleges in the nation. His professed procedure for academic progress is to conceive the major program ideas, delegating the matter of process to the dean of faculty and the usual committees. Asked whether such direct academic leadership on the president's part is accepted, he said, "Unless you do something preposterous, the faculty will tolerate a great deal. Not all the faculty members are in complete accord with this procedure, but they will accept it." A faculty member partially counters that statement: "He tends to keep his options open; he doesn't commit himself ahead of time. When he's impatient for a plan to win approval, then you know it is one that he really wants. But otherwise you don't know."

The other president believed in pushing her faculty members hard and pushing herself even harder. She seemed to be more liberal than they in moving for change, although her avowed preference was to let new ideas come from venturesome professors backed by experimental program grant money. She was known as accessible, pleasant, and businesslike. An economist with state university experience, she accepted disagreement as inherent in academic councils and won her share of issues in debate without resorting to autocracy. The general opinion was that "she's a good president." Some persons interviewed wished that "she could be better known on campus and perhaps relax a little more." She has since resigned this position to take on another position in public life—a position in higher education systems leadership.

Two remaining standard-bearer presidents have been grouped together because their institutions—one a private liberal arts college, the other a private university of 10,000 students—are elite institutions with top national reputations. The question for such favored persons might be, What's left to do?

Top executives like to honor themselves by referring to an inborn sense of discontent. College presidents who experience this discontent tend to put strong pressures on the institution to improve its reputation, whether the institution is near the top of the status ladder or several rungs down.

There are, however, some presidents who are content with their institution's status. Among the two standard bearer presidents not yet discussed, one came the closest to feeling downright satisfied with both his and his college's position. He also came the closest of all the presidents interviewed to confessing that he liked being a college president. Previously an academic dean, he feels close to curricular matters. He explained his adjustment to the presidential role:

> I spend a great deal of time looking at the appointment process.
> The faculty members, particularly those with tenure, are the main

> elements in providing stability and continued quality. My primary
> role as educator is making sure the best possible kinds of students
> are encouraged, compensated, and assisted. This role is subordi-
> nate to nothing, not even to the organization of curriculum.

He goes on to say that he delegates curriculum organization to the
committee on education policy or to the dean of the faculty.

President C. speaks of the constant variety, the chance to learn
from others (even from candidates for positions), the chance to watch
students develop, and the prodigal loyalty of the alumni. He evidently
holds to a Hobbesian view of university authority: "In a sense, all the
principal officers are members of the presidential staff. The more
autonomous officers are down the line." At one point, he described his
own role as a secular version of the role of the bishop who called
himself "the servant of the servants of God."[6]

The last of the standard-bearer presidents is President S., head of
the strong private university, and considerably less complacent than
the executive just described. For one thing, he must relate to the
directors of a complex of schools and colleges that includes a medical
center and a renowned center for international studies. The large
federal grants processed by the university bear constant watching and
raise intermittent controversy.

President S. was one of two of the twenty-five presidents who
speculated about the university president's diminished role as a
participant in national issues today. He saw this role as an obligation
incumbent on the presidents of major institutions and regretted that
he did not give more time to it: "I don't covet a national role, but I
would like to have an national audience for some things about higher
education that I think are worth saying."

The interviews with faculty members and students on this campus make interesting reading because they generally agreed that
President S. is doing a remarkable job, both collegially and mana-
gerially. His evident skill at inspiring followers to take on their own
leadership responsibilities—James MacGregor Burns's gospel of bona
fide leadership—mark his administration as one whose success invites
lengthier study. The only criticism of him, one directed at most
presidents, was that he spends a great deal of time off campus raising
money, at which he has been extremely successful.

President S. is occupied with overseeing large projects. As to his

6. Unfortunately, tapes containing faculty interviews at this institution were
lost. We have only the dean's comments, which closely corroborate the president's rather benign view.

role of instigating change in education, he is modest: "Very few of the really good ideas around here come from me. I do what I can to see that everybody else's good ideas get a hearing. Every once in a while, if the area is one about which I know relatively little, I get into difficulty with my adacemic peer leaders." Still he repudiates Cohen and March's thesis that unifying goals cannot exist.

The Organization President

Three of the presidents interviewed are categorized by the mundane term *organization president*. All three are presidents of universities (two public, one private). They are labeled such because they appear to be preoccupied with turning the gears of their complex machinery of schools, programs, and athletic teams with as little friction as possible and with a maximum output of graduates.

All three presidents have had considerable public administrative experience, ranging from experience on a Washington bureau to public relations work at a Western state university. All have earned doctorates (one has a Ph.D. in education).

In his initial statement, President Y. wrote at length about the leadership necessary for helping the institution plan for constrained growth:

> The first challenge, as I saw it, was to change the institution's mindset without having a devastating impact on the morale of the faculty and staff. The second was to try to work out a rational plan by which the physical plant could utilize space well enough to accommodate a maximum of 25,000 students.

President Y. went to some lengths to present himself as educating his large community in the arts and demands of administrative planning. The interview revealed that the president's leadership seemed more directly related to the older arts of political parlay and bargaining than to the introduction of innovative plans to solve educational dilemmas. Not long after our campus visit, a major administrative fracas followed the president's appointment of a provost who proceeded to ask for the resignations of many of the deans. The provost himself was at length relieved of his office.

The testimony gathered at this campus centered on how each problem had been thrashed out by a patient chief executive, whose working motto, according to one colleague, was "Confer, confer, confer." As a person, President Y. has been liked for his accessibility and his willingness to consult with groups, especially student groups, before taking action. But the president's great labor leaves the interviewer feeling that the use of personal diplomacy and political persuasion within the context of an unsettled and often turbulent state university system, rather than the leadership of his campus in major planning endeavors, became the identifying symbols of this executive officer. Students comment that he bore faith with them and brought them into the councils of debate. Yet the final impression is that the president in this situation had little chance for education statesmanship and that he would happily take on another assignment in his professional field (which has numerous lucrative outlets). His personal charm and his willingness to stay endlessly at the conference table won general approval, even warmth of feeling. Whether another administrator could bring more of an academic tone to a system fraught with politics was an unanswered question at the time of our interview.

The same question about executive character versus organizational environment was asked of President D., who heads a state university in the West. Before being appointed president of this institution, he had served as the president of a smaller state college. His earlier experience had been in public relations, including public relations for an athletics program. The faculty was quick to circulate the story that of the six candidates recommended to the regents, he was the last choice.

Sentiment toward President D. has changed remarkably in the last four years. He moved quickly to appoint as provost and academic administrator a well-regarded Eastern university graduate dean. The partnership has been well accepted. As the provost puts it: "We established a relationship that has caused no friction at all. The president expects me to operate the academic establishment. He expects to coordinate the overall areas himself and, of course, to be the university's representative to the public at all times." At the same time, the president made clear his own conviction about his role: "The president runs the campus because he is responsible for everything that goes on. I've heard people say that my role is external. But a president really can't be effective externally unless he or she is also deeply involved with what's happening on the campus." Of the political realities of his post he says, "In this state, the public is very close to the politicians. We know our governors and our senators and particularly our state legislators on a first-name basis."

The chairperson of the faculty senate, formerly a Yale professor, refers amicably to President D. by his nickname and tells anecdotes about him. At parties at the president's house, faculty members chat freely with him about "the politics of salary increases." Meanwhile, the campus has grown in number of programs and in general, large-scale attractiveness.

The organization presidents include one private university head, President T., whose former professional background was interrupted by service in a municipal post. His institution has a small endowment and is heavily dependent on tuition and fees. The institution, located at the edge of a metropolis, includes numerous professional schools and centers of continuing education. Most students in the area have not been exposed to high private tuition; thus, each annual price rise is a painful and anxious process.

Leadership must proceed on the basis of continual budget planning backed by board action. Faced with continued pressures, the president depends on a dedicated administrative team, often including the executive committee of the board: "I would not become president of an institution unless I believed that its administrators were competent and had initiative. Administrators, even more than faculty members, must show initiative."

President T. makes himself accessible to all those who feel strongly that they must confer with him; thus, at times, other academic authorities are bypassed. Of this procedure he says, "I don't offer it as an example of good presidential administration. I think it's largely a matter of personality. I believe I've got to be available to people and to carry through, rather than say, 'Let me consider this' or 'Let me discuss this with the dean.' "

President T. and his hard-pressed private university reflect trends that are becoming more difficult to deal with: enrollment and price competition, student retention, faculty tenure prospects, and relentlessly rising costs. Creative leadership is weighed down by the realities of costs and deficits. That President T.'s university recently won a national prize for innovative programming is encouraging, but it can hardly be relied on to bring major change.

President T. is outspoken about what a pragmatic administration must do. One of its first tasks must be to make decisions to help preserve solvency. Faculty members have criticized what they perceive to be shifting footwork and arbitrary presidential and board actions. To preserve shared governance, let alone faculty positions, at an institution under heavy financial challenge is an art that not many people want to learn. President T. speaks of a habit of sensitivity to the feelings of others: "Whether or not I can take the drastic measures that clearly have to be taken and not be hypersensitive to the hostility of the faculty is going to be a good test for me."

The Moderator President

The leadership style of the moderator president is reminiscent of that of the moderator of an egalitarian society and can be traced to the traditions of liberal Protestant churches in America and of the New England town meeting.[7] This style is difficult to adapt to complex institutions with multiple schools. Of the presidents we interviewed, only one, President G., might be classified as a true moderator president. He was the president of an institution in northern New England, and his role has been described earlier in this chapter as an administrator who had learned the art of delegating and of consulting on policy with a willingness to change his mind when faced with sufficient evidence from his faculty and student leaders.

Interviews with three of the presidents revealed a moderator style. In two cases, the results are not so impressive as they might be. In fact, one president has now resigned after a brief term in office. In defense of his own style, he pointed out that at both institutions where he had served as president he had to assume considerable authority because of budget limitations on granting faculty tenure. In his description of his responsibilities, he lists continued conferences with department heads and committees. He was known to be extremely accessible, both informally and by appointment.

As with most classifications, this categorizing of presidential leadership styles can distort the role of an actual president on an actual campus. The moderator president is particularly hard to pin down because the term has two different connotations. It may refer to a person who has fully thought through what goals he or she desires and is organized well enough to lead the community toward these goals. The term may also refer to someone who feels called upon to improvise, keeping channels open and the sails readied for a favorable breeze. We encountered both types in our interviews.

President H., who showed as much vacillation as moderating skill, asserted, "The president has had to take a very strong position on a number of matters." That statement was corroborated by the academic dean. The interviews with faculty members, students, and other staff members gave a less incisive view of the executive leadership. All agreed that President H. was friendly, informal, and highly accessible. Many, however, thought that his goals for the college were not well defined; the phrase "ad hoc" was used several times to

7. See Alexander W. Astin and Rita A. Scherrei's remarks about egalitarian presidents in *Managing Colleges for Maximum Effectiveness* (San Francisco: Jossey-Bass, 1979).

describe his objectives. A senior professor said, "I have never really had any discussions with him in which a strong philosophy of education has come through." Another said, "I don't think the president gets actively involved in matters of education."

The students interviewed were unusually vague about this president's positions. All they knew was that he wanted to put the college on a stronger footing and that, presumably because of his fund-raising activities, he was often absent from the campus.

President H. was praised from several quarters for his above-board style and his willingness to be persuaded. Moreover, he seemed inclined to respond to personal appeals that came to him directly rather than through channels.

President H.'s statements offer some insight into some problems of a young college that has not yet built a base firm enough to offer a solid curriculum equal to its competition. Leadership to carry out that task requires, among other things, a strong board and genuine regional support. The need to provide continual leadership, both on campus and off, has discouraged dozens of college presidents; they wonder how one person can be expected to provide both kinds of leadership simultaneously and with charisma, wisdom, and the strength and hide of an elephant.

The second moderator president, President F., heads a college almost completely different from the institution just described. His college is regarded as one of the best centers of undergraduate arts and sciences in the country; it has excellent resources, a traditionally strong faculty, and a long record of self-sufficiency. Given the institution's credentials, we had expected the president to be the confident leader of a confident enterprise. Because he is president of an institution where, for many years, both faculty and students have shared in the governance, we had assumed that he would be a moderate in administrative matters.

The interview began with President F.'s assertion that, while the question of the president's role as a leader in education is a timely one, the administrative priorities present a continual problem: "The managerial demands are extraordinary, even in a small college." His only escape from being "just a systems manager," he said, was working with key policy committees—promotion and tenure, and resource use—and with an all-college council on education policy. "I think we have done the necessary things soberly and effectively. That's what presidents like to hope." He asked his own question: "How is the president *educating*—in the European sense of the word and in the nineteenth-century American liberal arts college sense of the word? I educate chiefly through private conversations, public speeches, and such symbolic activities as helping coach an athletic team."

Others interviewed at that institution indicated more explicitly that they had expected President F. to show more direct leadership on policy issues but had been disappointed. He forms a close team with the provost. The provost apparently agrees with the president that education leadership should come "by slow degrees." The provost also feels that "the managerial model of leadership would result in poor morale because we don't manufacture pots and pans."

On the other hand, students and faculty members perceived hesitancy in the president's stance that bothered and, to an extent, frustrated them. One said, "I get the picture of a person who's not quite comfortable being the boss." A senior professor expressed nostalgia for a former president: "He would consult widely and ask for advice, but he alone would make the the ultimate decision. The president today has many constituents whose rights he has to consider, and yet within these bounds it is certainly possible for a president to exercise leadership that will be recognized and not resented." Even students proposed, "During the past ten years we've had a terrible fear of antidemocracy. As a result, consensus has been the desired mode of operation, but it's not a good idea now—people don't know what they want."

At another institution, widely agreed to be a strong school, faculty and students who were interviewed unexpectedly concurred that stronger signals from the top were seriously needed. The double bind of the president's role was again illustrated: leadership must "come slowly," yet if it does not occur in ways that can be identified (and, to be sure, perhaps contested), the strong institution as well as the weaker one may drift.

Similar disadvantages of the moderator leadership style surfaced at another college, likewise a well-regarded center of able faculty and students with a tradition of campus democracy. Here President W. lives amid memories of a recently departed executive who, during a long tenure, had established a tradition of being directly involved in most institutional policy issues. During his administration, the faculty—even its stronger members—deferred to him.

Now in his fourth year, President W. is establishing his own moderating style. It differs from that of the hesitant President F. in that it proposes solutions to a question and then defers the decision until the academic community has been consulted. To some constituents, this procedure indicates that the president is dodging leadership. To others, it is an acceptable use of the moderator technique; moreover, it is important that the president's preference always be made clear. When asked whether the eventual decision would be known as President W.'s decision, the president responded, "No, it will be called an administrative council decision. It won't have my name on it. It won't be personalized."

We left this institution with the impression that the vote was still out on whether this president (then in his fourth year) had achieved a balance between personal leadership and due regard for the opinions of leading figures on campus and in the community. The faculty members who were interviewed agreed that he was less sure of getting results than his predecessor had been. Still they noted that the former president sometimes got his wishes through a certain indirection, whereas President W. is more forthright. Furthermore, President W. works through, rather than around, the governance bodies: "One thing I particularly respect about him is that he has passed up several opportunities to be a hero."

The Explorer President

The term *explorer president* was chosen after more heroic names had been eliminated. Even the word *explorer* connotes qualities that may require some modification. The contemporary college president's lexicon has no word for the man or woman who is able singlehandedly to create a unique institution, much less sustain it.

The explorer president takes on the personal challenge of bringing concrete change to his or her institution. The change may be substantive or it may be organizational, but in both cases the purpose of change is to call attention to an existing need unmet by the institution.

One explorer president, President J., used his formidable experience in the hard sciences to devise a plan whereby the college, by deliberately requiring one summer term in the four-year course, was physically able to accommodate, without having to build major new facilities, a student body 20 percent larger than before. The trustees and the alumni council previously had been strongly opposed to the admission of women into this student body. The president's plan, however, would keep the percentage and numbers of men from declining because the summer enrollment obviated the need for new residence halls for women. As a result, the plan was approved.

President X., head of a large metropolitan college comprising a wide variety of programs, undertook to introduce an interdisciplinary program of studies in aging. In so doing, she not only crossed swords with deans and chairpersons representing the several disciplines but also launched the college's first interdisciplinary program. The first year she ran the seminar herself, for two reasons: first, "to learn a good deal about it so that I could support it," and second, "to see if we could establish a truly interdisciplinary program. It seemed to me that only if I ran the seminar for a year could I convince the academic community that no one owned this turf."

The third explorer president in our sample, President N., came from a second-echelon post in a very prestigious private university to the presidency of a public university in a small state. Budgetary problems were threatening the institution, which was not well supported by the state legislature. With a small team of vice presidents, President N. took on the task of reducing by half an overstaffed administration while giving the academic departments the facts about fiscal stringency. At the same time, he persuaded the academic administration to build programs of general education while tightening faculty tenure and promotion. President N. has presided, not as a take-charge president, but out of an apparent conviction that forthright leadership can inspire others in an institution that has lagged behind in presenting education as the management of change. Currently his proposals face some faculty resistance; time will tell whether his efforts will be successful. He may have to learn to be patient and to develop a rhythm that is closer to the rhythm of his present region than that of the region he left.

President E., the fourth explorer president, heads one of the largest single campuses in the nation. He is the first to concede that when he walks the university paths, hardly one student in ten can identify him. Two other presidents at universities of comparable size in our sample face the same situation. President E.'s response to the problem of personal anonymity varies from the others, however: he does not pop into student cafeterias or entertain students en masse but concentrates instead on meeting with elected student leaders regularly for lunch.

President E. believes that the president of a megaversity has a responsibility to embody in a concrete way the expectations that a center of higher learning ought to have for its constituents—students, faculty members, and administrators alike.

> I think that leadership involves the willingness to take a strong position, even with the full knowledge that one might lose. As presidents, we all accept certain aspects of university life that we

don't personally enjoy—for example, having to deal with the issues of big-time intercollegiate athletics or insisting on honesty, no matter what the program—because we know that the alternative is flat-out resignation. Another ancient virtue of "leadership management" that counts for a great deal is integrity. When I discovered that an applicant admitted to a select professional school was admitted solely because of his political connections, I met with each dean separately, looked them in the baby blues (as they say), and said,"We're not going to have that."

This account may sound a little self-righteous, but President E. has followed his own rhetoric by taking on several thorny issues. For example, he challenged the code of private practice privileges for clinical professors in the medical center, with explosive results. The president's comment: "I've laid my job right out on the line with this one." He has also tackled the promotion review practices of department chairpersons, the procedure for searching for deans of the various schools, and even the selection of a new dormitory director. Concerning the search for a state system chancellor, he said, "I feel about chancellors the way I feel about university presidents: there's no compelling evidence that a good one makes much difference, but there *is* compelling evidence that a bad one makes a hell of a lot of difference."

President E.'s efforts to set standards of personal integrity for the university's administrative staff apparently have made a mark. A senior administrator says, "Simply by being a spokesperson, he has given the university a new self-respect and a national visibility that it did not enjoy before." Several faculty members credit him with broadening the university's image from that of a mainly local institution to that of a national one. The provost, rather than the president, is generally acknowledged to guide education policy itself. The president of the faculty organization, which is officially an adversary group, stated that President E., compared with his predecessors, has been "a marvelous improvement." The interviews indicate that the president has deliberately taken on tough issues and that he has worked to broaden the university's image.

The data gathered from the interviews at this institution mark President E. as an executive of a large, impersonal organization who has explored ways of providing his organization with a framework of personal values. This approach, which could be considered an exploration of large-scale management possibilities, might also serve as model for humanizing large institutions. If the president sets the pace in that direction and holds out for integrity while trying to resolve problems, then he or she is providing education leadership in a particularly sensitive area, the realm of values.

The Founding President

The last president interviewed is a type more rare today than in earlier years: the founding president. In our sample, the founding president was the chancellor of a campus within a state system. The founding president has played a large role in American college history. Cowley's designation for the period 1870–1910, "the Age of the Titans," has been mentioned earlier. Clark Kerr, in the much-quoted *Uses of the University*, gives such early leaders full credit while noting that they were often targets of ferocious opposition led by vituperative geniuses such as Thorstein Veblen and Upton Sinclair. Yet the dividing issues were simpler in the days before ultraspecialization and federal subsidies in the 1960s incited the academic revolution, the revolt of the faculty.[8]

In recent times, numerous institutions (usually private) with a special mission have been founded and particular educators selected to head them. Every decade seems to produce its New College or equivalent somewhere in the United States.

The special-mission institution that we visited was experiencing a problem which, while not unusual, presented a certain irony. The institution's mission had centered on an environment-based, interdisciplinary liberal arts curriculum. Recently, the institution had come up against decreasing enrollment and regional pressures for a more conventional curriculum featuring career-based sequences such as business administration. One senior faculty member noted that from the start the project had to fight an up-hill battle because the region was so conservative. Of the chancellor he said, "One of his goals was to relate this university to the community, and I think that goal continues to be an important one. Unfortunately, because the university is not a product of the region but was superimposed on it, the relationship between the university and the local community is somewhat artificial." Other faculty members agreed that the institution and the region were mismatched. Students were equally perceptive: "The problem right now is that this university seems to be trying to make itself more traditional because that's what the local community wants. Enrollment has fallen off, and there is a budget bind."

8. See Christopher Jencks and David Riesman, *The Academic Revolution* (New York: Doubleday, 1968).

Reporting procedure for the innovations at this institution no longer ends with the chancellor; in fact, it moves in the other direction. The chain of reporting may reflect the chancellor's position as father of a new educational enterprise, yet it also makes evident that the enterprise is no longer under his official act of approval. The chancellor's remarks during a long interview reflected this change. Instead of talking about his program, he talked about budget strategy and governance procedures. Instead of forecasting a future spent guiding the program he had started a dozen years before, he spoke of referring curriculum policy through the faculty to the dean. (A vice chancellor for academic affairs, formerly the chancellor's alter ego, has left his position and has not been replaced.) Of the members of the faculty senate the chancellor said, "They elect their own chairperson. They are a very independent group, so independent that whenever I meet with them, I go to their office; they don't come to mine." (Other interviews indicated that the chancellor is now known to prefer a certain formality of relationships, even though in earlier days at the institution he and his planning staff had reached decisions informally.)

The chancellor expressed disappointment with the low level of responsibility taken by student government. Formerly, he implied, he had relied on student initiative, and he regretted that when the institution changed the all-university requirements that year, "it was done without any student input." Still, of the students as individuals, he said, "They're a fantastic bunch; they want the administration, the faculty, and the students to be more vigilant in deliberating about the academic plan."

The interview ended on a discursive, philosophic note, with the chancellor contrasting the joys of creating a new institution with the depressing effects of a declining budget on the imaginative spirit. His closing comments concerned human needs for self-renewal. He spoke of the uplift that he experienced from delving into a new field of interest, in this case ornithology, in his off hours. The subject of his university's founding mission was not mentioned again.

In this culminating interview, we had an unusual opportunity to view a president who has been celebrated as an innovative leader but who subsequently has been forced by changing circumstances to withdraw from that role. Clearly, one solution would be for him to change positions, but, as happens in many cases, the right change of position had not come along. The problem of the mature administrator who takes office filled with creative ideas is that the ideas carry a certain time limit. The best of novel curricular plans in the American college lose currency after a period of years; other ideas move in to supersede them. The problem is part of the phenomenon of leadership in higher education and is not uncommon throughout the country.

Recapitulation: Power and Personality

The foregoing account of how college and university presidents see themselves and how they are seen ought to indicate something about how organizations respond to persons who have been chosen to lead. Some questions—for example, whether or not education was conducted differently at that institution because of that particular individual's actions—would require additional research.

The effects of a president's actions are difficult to measure, even by people who have lived and worked with the president on the same campus at the same time. The purpose of the Presidency Project was to record both the intentions of the presidents and their reactions to their leadership. Any measurement of change, up to the level of a "transforming leadership," is limited to tangible evidence of college progress (or regress) directly attributable to the president. Changes in college procedure or organization instituted by the president could not be recorded during our brief visits, although a few of these were discussed.

What is more relevant to our purpose is to see in the testimony of administrators, faculty members, and students the dynamics of personal power, by which presidents of colleges and universities— including even large, complex organizations—can influence events, if not determine them. The fact that some persons interviewed exaggerated the real extent of this power does not diminish it, since belief itself can be a potent force in preserving the mystique of the presidency. It can also discourage other campus groups from entering into a role in decision making. Folklore to the contrary, it is easier than it should be for a president to decide a policy matter alone and usher it past the trustees on to the faculty and students.

Presidents bring about change in various ways and through various leadership styles. By definition, the take-charge president makes decisions. President B., the young, upcoming president of a small college in need of recharging, has exemplified the first category. The board is enthusiastic, faculty are grateful for financial stabilization, and the president's constituency—including students—concedes broad power.

Standard-bearer presidents, our second category, can gain headway by tightening standards even further and building toward the happy event of a student market that becomes virtually inelastic. With such a base there is room for an occasional easing of policy, as in the case of the standard-bearer president who supported alumni efforts to bolster intercollegiate athletics. These presidents' biggest question: What is our ultimate goal?

Organization presidents are sufficiently well defined by their classification title to require little further analysis. The most successful learn the machinery well enough to produce large, sound universities after a period has passed in which the institution may have been disorganized and faltering. Mid-level organization presidents bring stability and hard work to unstable situations. The least inspiring executives of this class offer transactional leadership that accomplishes the essential business of degree-producing while the institution gathers forces for the next thrust into new programs and better procedures.

Moderator presidents may be leaders who as often as not are seen as uncertain administrators too ready to delegate decisions. Properly prepared, they can become skillful organizers of community thought. Some are suspected of manipulating or lobbying behind the scenes to ensure that the "right" decisions are made. Half of the moderator presidents in our sample demonstrated their skill at mixing open debate with personal persuasion to achieve rational decisions made through a reasonably democratic process.

The success of a moderator president depends on using good timing to introduce relevant facts that lead to sensible decisions. A hang-up over democratic process can lead to disenchantment: "If the president can't speak his own mind, why are we expected to do it for him?"

Successful explorer presidents evidence signs of having their act together. That act includes playing the role of chief instigator without false modesty. The explorer president ideally combines the zeal of the pioneer with the canny perception of an advance scout among alien tribes.

Presidents who explore too many directions at once may lose the confidence of their constituents. Explorers also run the risks of getting lost, being defeated by larger forces, or being bypassed when conditions radically change. Yet they present the most attractive answer to two questions that have underscored the Presidency Project: (1) Can a president lead an institution in such a way that he or she makes a difference? and (2) Is the position of president, whatever the level of the institution, worth holding in present times?

The explorer presidents whom we interviewed, while differing in almost every way, gave us a consistent answer to these questions. Their responses can be paraphrased: "I'm here because I think I can make a difference. The job is, first, one of good management, yet it is management in which people are the prime concern. Beyond management, the responsibility is to see that this institution grows internally, changes, experiments, and leads."

5 The Future Presidential Setting

Campuses and College Systems

"A rose is a rose is a rose is a rose," Gertrude Stein's famous definition, is now accepted as conventional wisdom. However, this wisdom is not applicable to colleges and universities. Educators are only beginning to realize how greatly teaching and student response to that teaching are shaped by certain ecological factors, namely, the institutional setting. One of the requirements of the job of president, as important as any other, is an understanding of these facts of ecology.

The birth of the behavioral sciences, a means of classifying certain kinds of knowledge, may prove to be one of the quietly important achievements in education during the latter twentieth century. Lay people and more than a few educators still trip over the difference between *behavioral* and *behavioristic*. The term *behaviorial* is used to describe the many ways in which disciplines that observe human beings in individual and group action relate to one another. Behavioral interactions are being usefully applied in the study of personal development vis-à-vis the environmental impact on students and students' response to their environment.

Over time, the geographic setting of colleges and universities contributes to the perceived character of the institution. For example, Dartmouth College's folklore of outdoorsmanship is so pervasive that its president is expected to manifest, in spirit if not in action, a zest for overnight group hikes and the powder snows of a five-months' New England winter. Some institutions, such as Reed College and the University of Chicago, put environmental elements together and eliminate distractions such as intercollegiate athletics and fraternities in ways that enhance intellectual growth. At other institutions, an atmosphere of anti-intellectualism, anti-institutionalism, or impersonality may prevail. Such kinds of atmospheres have ways of persisting on a campus. Even though higher education is gradually becoming more cosmopolitan, the local flavor of individual institutions still needs to be studied. Because educators will continue to deal with human beings and not machine tools, the educational process will continually confront surprises along the way—surprises calling for the best adaptive efforts on the part of those who teach, learn, or administer at that institution.

Colleges and universities must face the inevitable truth that they, as settings of human events in a rapidly changing society, are also changing. This fact should be obvious enough, yet many sponsors of traditional institutions, such as colleges and churches, often resent these changes. Presidents, like pastors, are caught between the inexorable outside pressures for change and their patrons' insistence that change be resisted. To persons who have an investment in keeping things substantially as they are, education as well as religion presents dilemmas when change is called for. The demand on the leader to bring his or her constituency face to face with change could possibly bring forth a transforming leadership, depending on how resourceful the leader is in making evident the personal benefits of change.

Other changes are not beneficial, and adapting to these changes requires leadership of another sort. The most conspicuous change in higher education organization during the past two decades is the growth of college and university systems—the development of state networks under central control for the purpose of coordinating institutional planning at the two-year college level, the four-year college level, and the university level. (California has the most fully developed system for all three levels.)

Independent institutions, in an effort to widen their influence and following, have sporadically established branch campuses. In some cases, branch campuses have been extended virtually nationwide; an example is Antioch College (though it has recently reduced the geographic dispersal of its units). In some thirty-five states, the coordination of all or almost all public higher education is headed by a single state agency.[1] Several large state university systems—such as those in California, New York, Pennsylvania, and North Carolina—have been under central control of university centers located around the state.

Four of the presidents interviewed for the Presidency Project lead universities that are part of a state system. Typically, perhaps, the degree of autonomy among the four varies. At these campuses, the chief executive's title varies also; at some institutions it is "president,"

---

1. Education Commission of the States, *Challenge, Coordination, and Governance in the 1980's* (Denver, Colo.: ECS, 1980).

at others "chancellor." This variation reflects in a small way the states' power in making policy for higher education in this country.

The question of title is of minor concern compared with the question of how much authority is to be delegated to the branch campus and how much is to be retained by the president (or chancellor) at the system headquarters. The issue goes beyond details of protocol. Is the head of a branch campus responsible for long-range planning, budget formation, or major changes in program? If the executive of the branch campus bears a second-level title—such as "provost," or, as in Pennsylvania, "director"—what is his or her relationship to the faculty? The president of a university whose campuses have proliferated over several towns, counties, or even states will require a new kind of administrative lieutenancy if he or she expects to cast any lasting influence over the course of events on each campus.

Once the relationships of officers to the institutional system have been made clear, the president will probably care little about the title that designates the position. In Great Britain and Europe, the college head may have any number of names, according to the ecclesiastical tradition of the particular college—"master," "warden," "president," "rector," or "principal." Still the prerogatives of the single campus are made clear. At a conference some years ago, Oxford dons iterated the three ancient rights of the individual colleges that make up Oxford University: the right to admit their own students, the right to appoint and retain their own faculty, and the right to choose their courses of study. Presidents of university and college systems in America might do well to take note.

For the period ahead, the American college president needs more concrete guidelines about which policy decisions are to rest with the individual college or university and which are to rest with the central administration. Clearly, these guidelines are bound up with the organization of the central board of trustees and with whatever counterpart body of lay persons, if any, vested with whatever specified power, oversees each campus unit. The crux of the matter is organization, since the president of any learning center normally obtains his or her own power from that local authority.

In New York, thirty individual college and university councils representing state-operated units of SUNY are accorded one statutory power, the nomination of the local president. In one instance, this one power was abrogated by the central SUNY board. Whatever the merits and flaws of the system, the message seems clear: in a systems organization, the prospective presidential nominee—and the faculty and boards— will need to know where the president's campus powers begin and end. The faculty and the boards must know it also.

The organization of a national framework of higher education, which now enrolls twelve million students and which ten years from now may enroll several millions fewer (or, if the development of new markets offsets the effect of dropping birth curves, millions more), is due for continued change. Around the nation the loosely organized (one might say disorganized) arrangement of systems, half systems, and lack of systems, along with the private sector's contending with different bases of followers and finances, points toward the construction of more efficient systems to represent what is optimistically labeled the diversity of American higher education.

When all has been said, at least half the future presidents will operate on a campus that is essentially single, private, and autonomous, insofar as mounting state and federal oversight will permit. (The heavy proportion of enrollment in the public sector—80 percent—tends to obscure the fact that there are still more private institutions than public institutions in the United States.) The idea of the college cluster—exemplified by the Claremont Colleges and the Atlanta University Center—relies on agreement that each tub will stand on its own bottom. In such places, rivalry is as strong as cooperation. For single-campus presidents, then, systems organization will come either through voluntary collegiate associations for mutual aid or through state efforts such as the promotion of regionalism, something that New York, for instance, has tried from time to time.

The results of the Presidency Project reveal that personalized leadership is desired at all institutions. Such leadership denotes a quality of attention to individuals and indicates a need for administrators who are able to deal more openly with those who teach, learn, and create (see Chapter 3). The day-to-day operations of leading a single-campus center of higher learning may require of these presidents skills different from the equally necessary skills of the managers of university systems. The successful transition of presidents from the leadership of universities to that of smaller institutions suggests a desire and a talent for personalized leadership, which undoubtedly influences some leaders to make such a move. For example, during the 1950s Rufus Harris moved from Tulane University to Mercer University, and two years ago, Eugene Mills moved from the University of New Hampshire to Whittier College.

Other presidents with a talent for personal effectiveness have chosen to work within large institutions. Their skills may include the ability to work effectively in one-on-one situations. They cannot rely only on charisma from the podium, a style better suited to the brilliant lecturer than to the executive, who may have to spend several hours in give-and-take conferences with high-placed colleagues on details of governance involving many institutions. Still, such presidents relate primarily to the system as a whole, not to individual schools or colleges.

The requirements of leadership of a large public university are different in kind as well as in degree from those of a smaller college, where the chief administrator may feel personally close to the institution and to his or her colleagues. If a large institution is to feel some effect of leadership, it needs either a conspicuous institutional success (e.g., a major scientific discovery) or, at the least, a visible and audible chief executive who advances the claims of the university through the media as well as through the inner political processes within the state capitol. Selective attention to the most urgent problem becomes part of the president's style. The university president must protect himself or herself from being dragged into an athletic recruiting scandal, for example; if such a scandal does occur, that onus can be borne by emphasizing the larger picture of what the university is doing and by setting the errors of an over-zealous football coach in perspective. The test, as Harold L. Enarson, of The Ohio State University, has said, comes when the president realizes that he or she is now the standard representative of a great place of learning.[2]

Leadership of higher education has become specialized, both because of the scope of organization required for the education of millions and because of the special aspects of different education settings. (In industry, specialization of leadership has led to the rise of group management.) If Cowley's titan presidents are no more to be found, the loss to student learning and human development may not be irreplaceable. What remains is the accent on education leadership as a human activity consistent with the human elements of the learning process itself.

The future settings of American higher education will probably not be more simple or more personalized. Efforts to capture the human elements of the college experience—for example, through arrangements of decentralized organization and more representative governance procedures—can, perversely enough, defeat their own aims.[3] Thus, if colleges and universities in the future are to hold on to

2. Personal interview with Enarson, April 1978.

3. See Virginia B. Smith and Alison R. Bernstein, *The Impersonal Campus: Options for Reorganizing Colleges to Increase Student Involvement, Learning, and Development* (San Francisco: Jossey-Bass, 1979).

the human interchange that is the essence of liberal education, it is increasingly important that incoming presidents understand what must be done to separate, even defend, the community of the single campus from the multicampus system. Maintaining this human interchange was a prominent concern of at least a third of the presidents interviewed, and that number would have been greater had not more than a third of the twenty-five institutions been private colleges independent of a systems connection.

Today there is no realistic argument against the continuing growth of state systems. (The plea that liberal education requires a cottage industry mentality is a sentimentalism.) In the future, presidents of all institutions—whatever the size or organization scheme—will face changes in structure, clientele, and purpose as well as in content. Our comments on the nature of systems presidencies versus campus presidencies are meant to underscore the fact that American colleges and universities vary widely in their approaches to stability and that, regardless of preference, in the future they will undoubtedly be occupied more extensively with both state and federal coordination. Boards and committees should bear these developments in mind as they seek in the future to match top administrative posts with the training and skills of men and women who can be most effective in them.

Faculty Today, Faculty Tomorrow

Many a president has remarked, particularly after a Monday plenary faculty meeting, that there is no one on earth so independent or so loath to change as a senior professor, especially one who happens not to be a chairperson. A few years ago, Princeton University appointed a committee to review its undergraduate program of liberal arts. After nearly a year of study involving a book-length series of proposals for changes in both content and form, the committee carefully voted down each of its proposals, declaring in conclusion that the university's undergraduate program was quite satisfactory as it was.

A faculty member's stance toward education, however, may be less reserved within his or her own office or among more intimate colleagues. During the past decade, the phrase *faculty development* has gained a guarded sort of credence. The recession of 1970–71, with its tightening budgets, new tenure rigors, and so forth, instigated a gradual increase in faculty members' interest in widening academic competence to include fields cognate to their own. Department retrenchments brought on by legislative cutbacks and, in private institutions, by uncertain finances have led untenured faculty members to consider changing fields altogether. Faculty members who have passed through institutional purgatory into tenure show new attention to faculty development, partly because of the stimulus of the federal Fund for the Improvement of Postsecondary Education and partly because of management contracts containing retrenchment clauses that cause even tenured professors to feel threatened by a prospective sharp drop in the university's instruction budget. Administrators, meanwhile, pay serious attention to limiting or reducing the percentage of the faculty eligible to hold tenure in the institution.

That faculties today are ready to embrace change would be an inaccurate signal to send to an incoming president. At its base the academic corporation changes little from decade to decade as far as its sense of intellectual autonomy is concerned. Burton Clark has observed a change in emphasis among faculty members:

> The major form of organization and authority found in the faculties . . . is now neither predominantly collegial nor bureaucratic. Difficult to characterize, it may be seen as largely "professional," but professional in a way that is critically different from the authority of professional men (and women) in other organizations such as the business corporation, the government agency, and the hospital. . . .[4]

Clark's analysis of this trend leads him to conclude:

> We are witnessing a strong trend toward a federated structure—with the campus more like a United Nations and less like a small town—and this trend affects faculty authority by weakening the faculty as a whole and strengthening the faculty in its many parts. . . .[5]

In light of this trend and the development of multicampus faculties attached to one central university or college, the president's task of appearing before the professoriate as the united body of the academic corporation becomes inappropriate and geographically unfeasible.

During the second half of the century, then, education leadership of an institution of higher learning has been characterized by one of two patterns of relationships between the president and the faculty. In part, these two kinds of relationships are natural developments of the separation of specialized professional and academic disciplines into distinct units within the university—an ancient tradition, as medieval historians point out, but one that developed much later in the United

4. Gary L. Riley and J. Victor Baldridge, eds., *Governing Academic Organizations: New Problems, New Perspectives* (Berkeley: McCutchan, 1977), p. 65.

5. Ibid., p. 75.

States. For more than two centuries, American colleges and universities followed the Cambridge-Oxford form of organization. American modes of organization emphasized the differences in the institutions' denominational background but had no counterpart for the overseeing university that conferred the degrees for all collegiate units. (The University of Toronto has followed the Oxbridge pattern, however.)

The leadership of the European university may be a strictly ceremonial position, like that of chancellor at British universities, or it may be an active administrative position (many rectors in continental universities are active administrators). In the British university system, the vice chancellors increasingly are operating like the presidents of American state university systems and are staying in office longer. Contacts with individual faculty members of constituent units are still mainly ceremonial, however, except when policy issues affecting the entire university, such as the issue of faculty unionization, must be resolved.

The future of faculty unions was clouded by the *Yeshiva* decision of 1980, presently under appeal, although several institutions have seized upon it to cancel their own union contracts. Thus far, the decision affects nonpublic institutions only, and the prediction still holds that public higher education will eventually enroll up to 85 percent or more of regularly enrolled students in the United States. Consequently, the increasing number of institutions electing to unionize may well portend future institutional and administrative life. That possibility is something that all new college presidents should ponder. Should they simply accept unionization, as leaders of industry do, or can some residue of collegiality still be coaxed into life?

The prospect of presiding over a built-in adversarial relationship with professional employees has not thus far reduced the lists of persons willing to become candidates for president. It has, however, changed attitudes on both sides about what degree of collegiality, if any, can be preserved between administrator and faculty members. In recent decades, this tradition of collegiality has been a compensation for college executives: industry executives, who enjoy much larger salaries, must accept a built-in hierarchical relationship with their colleagues, even their closest staff members. Frank Kemerer and Victor Baldridge concede that their study of campus unions made them more skeptical about the unions' effect on improving academic strength. They conclude:

> If higher education is to be healthier and stronger because of faculty collective bargaining, then it will require genuine states-

manship on all sides. . . . In the political battles to come there will be union members and administrators who are petty and contentious; there will also be . . . those in both camps who are creative leaders with goals of preserving the spirit of campus community. . . . In large measure, the fate of higher education depends on which style of leadership accompanies faculty collective bargaining.[6]

To become a "creative leader" of faculty members—who annually face lower salaries relative to the Consumer Price Index, decreasing funds for instruction, and increasing demands from the students for financial aid to offset rises in tuition—may scarcely sound like an opportunity to provide transforming leadership. If there were no prospects for improved governance, the challenge of leading the faculty today could be compared at best to the challenge to a gladiator.

Whatever the effect on higher education, most faculty members seem to cherish above all else the freedom to create their own academic life and to be appreciated—to be praised by the academic community for scholarly individual accomplishment or for creative teaching and, as well, to be rewarded with promotions and salary increases. At the present time there are signs that the professoriate's interests have swung to the larger problems of society, such as the world surge in biogenetics, whose implications for attacking scientific and human problems seem endless. Higher learning is becoming increasingly important to human survival in a universe whose mysteries daily broaden, and an executive who gets involved in higher education at this time may be joining the academic community in one of the most exciting epochs since the university was born.

The interviews of the Presidency Project, as previous chapters have made clear, revealed an expected degree of faculty skepticism that modern university presidents can or should attempt to be education leaders beyond setting major policies and conditions. Even productive scholars who have recently become presidents are said to lose touch with developments in their field at a rate approaching the square of the time that has elapsed since they were full-fledged scholars. The condescension displayed by some faculty members toward this kind of president—"He's not a scholar in the real sense"—was counterbalanced by the belief expressed by other faculty members that these presidents were interested in supporting academic life.

6. Frank R. Kemerer and Victor J. Baldridge, *Unions on Campus: A National Study of the Consequences of Faculty Bargaining* (San Francisco: Jossey-Bass, 1975), p. 233.

New presidents should know a few other things about their faculty members: the percentage, by fields, of untenured faculty members; the representation and academic status of faculty members of minority groups or ethnic origin; and the number, fields, rank, and salary distribution of women. The last two items were reviewed with special care in 1978-79 by the Sloan Commission on Government and Higher Education, as a later section of this chapter reports. The affirmative action program has become a symbol of overhanging controversy between colleges and the federal government, and a few institutions have chosen to take outright issue with the program.

In the future the most problematic issue that incoming chief executives will face will probably be the often peremptory challenge that could be presented at any time by any faculty segment struggling for equitable treatment regardless of sex, race, religious preference, or probationary faculty status. In 1978-79, for example, women full professors averaged $2,600 less than men full professors.[7] In fall 1976 (the latest year reported), the total number of women instructional faculty members was 175,000, while the total number of men instructors was 466,000.[8] (In the United States today, there are 2 percent more women than men.)

Obviously no future generation of presidents can expect to change these facts and conditions in one wave of action. These chapters have presented contemporary colleges and universities as they exist— varied communities of men and women ranging widely in age, status, and aspiration. The faculty members form the institution's character as a center of education.

The status of faculty members within the hierarchy of higher education has changed a great deal in some ways since the early twentieth century. The same can be said of presidents. One thing does not change, however, as data from our study confirm: the success with which the president and the faculty stabilize their expectations of each other will, more than anything else, determine the effectiveness of the institution they serve. And the converse is equally true.

Students in the 1980s

Once upon a time the president was something like Mr. Chips. He (most presidents were male) was known as "Prexy." He could be

7. *Digest of Education Statistics 1980* (Washington, D.C.: National Center for Education Statistics, 1980), p. 107.

8. Charles J. Andersen, comp. *1980 Fact Book for Academic Administrators* (Washington, D.C.: American Council on Education, 1980), p. 116.

benign, paternal, paternalistic. In the not so remote past, he taught religion or theology courses, or he might have given a special course on virtue.

Today the president's visibility and his or her closeness to the students varies among institutions, but both are obviously functions of the size of the institution. A student could spend four years at an institution, particularly a large institution, without ever having laid eyes on the president. As one of the presidents in our study put it: "The way the president is perceived is almost entirely a function of what appears in the paper." A student said of this president: "I would describe him as a mystery. I know he exists because I've seen him, but that's about it."

Almost no president knows enough about students, and most students know very little about the president's work. Clearly, this situation is not as it should be. Moreover, it reflects a general trend in modern bureaucratic society—a distance between government decisions and people's needs, thoughts, and feelings. Such remoteness is accompanied by symbolic presentations that suggest, more or less honestly, the leaders' concern for people's welfare and the inevitable distortions in people's minds of the complex problems their leaders face.

How can a president gain knowledge about students? Since the end of the 1960s, increasing numbers of books have been written about students. But more important than the information in these books is the process of obtaining that knowledge. There can be no substitute for first-hand acquaintance with student life, and presidents must make sufficient time for it. Presidents must observe students in the classrooms, in the dormitories, in the student union, and elsewhere. They must be accessible to students, both to elected student representatives and to more "random" students who will have to be sought out for informal chats, which can yield much important information. When serving as consultants on college campuses, we often found that after a day or two of interviewing students on a campus, we could tell the president things about the students' behavior and attitudes that he or she had not known, knowledge the president ought to have acquired on his or her own. If each president could at least occasionally teach a course, for example, he or she would acquire some unusual first-hand knowledge of students as well as a better understanding of what the faculty is up against. But given the burden of the job, this expectation may be unrealistic. Moreover, unless the president is sufficiently conversant in a particular subject, faculty members may be skeptical about the seriousness of his or her teaching effort.

One president in our sample has gone further than others to gather knowledge about his students:

> I have deliberately structured the university's organization so that I am more involved in student affairs. All the academic deans report to me through the provost. The only exception is the vice president for student affairs, who reports to me directly, because I want to be more directly involved with student affairs. Also, I still teach a course—European history since 1848—so I get to meet the students in my class. The dean of students arranges for me to have monthly luncheons with a group of student leaders. I go to the union to have coffee, stand around, and meet people. I try to make a point of having student groups to the house. I try to keep up with the students, particularly those in leadership positions, but also with others. Sometimes I go uninvited to spend an evening in a dormitory.

Another president in our sample has started a system of having students serve as interns in administrative offices.

A president who knows students only through the research and other literature is besieged with a mass of often contradictory and outdated information. Nothing is more easily dated these days than reports about students: ever since the end of World War II, if not before, student attitudes have been changing rapidly. Sometimes, of course, the "newness" of current students can be exaggerated.

Students reflect both variant and invariant characteristics. The invariant characteristics change relatively little. Students, particularly between the ages of 17–22, go through fairly regular cycles of development, often beginning with brash dogmatism and ending with a more mature sense of the complexity and endless corrigibility of scientific and personal beliefs. In between these two stages are fairly regular patterns of rebellion, lack of self-esteem, and identity confusion, and more or less movement toward independence, integrity, and capacity for caring relationships with others.

These invariant characteristics need attention. If the college or university conceives its role as the transfer of information, it will neglect the cultivation of the emotional and social capacities by which information is acquired, sifted, and critically assimilated. In the end, the institution will not even succeed in transferring much desirable information beyond the day of the final examination. The invariant characteristics hold for the "new" student as well. Nowadays there is a larger number of older undergraduates than in the past. These older students have more experience, but in a different way they can be as dogmatic as 17-year-old freshmen, and the struggles with identity and self-validation are by no means over.

Among the specters haunting the college or university president in the 1980s is the vocational orientation of students. Periodically, the traditional liberal arts are declared dead, sometimes with glee and sometimes with sorrow. Institutions are viewed as training grounds for jobs in industry and business—jobs that are often downgraded, with college graduates now doing work once reserved for high school graduates. In some sense, administrators and faculty members have become the victims of their own rhetoric. Nobody talked nearly as much about job preparation in the 1960s when jobs were more plentiful. Now job preparation is being emphasized as if the problem were preparation and not the conditions of the labor market itself. A further complicating factor is that, while some fields are over-crowded, others still offer opportunities—and students often do not know which is which.

All this is not to say that colleges and universities should not help prepare students for the job market. Jobs and job prospects are important to students, and their motivation and willingness to work while in college will in many ways depend on what their sense of their future is. But in the rush to be au courant in the 1980s, many institutions have neglected to consider that students come to college for many reasons in addition to preparing themselves for good jobs. Research over a long period of time has shown that students as well as alumni highly value the nonpragmatic knowledge they acquire in college. One student told us that students on his campus are becoming "concerned with the way that a certain department stresses the need for developing a skill that students can market as opposed to the study of liberal arts." Moreover, he warned, such emphasis could result in a higher student attrition rate.

Depending on their predilections, students may find as much or more fulfillment in literature, art, and the social or natural sciences as in sports, hobbies, or crafts. Students also continue to say they expect that a college education will help them develop a philosophy of life, psychological self-knowledge, and ways of getting to know people and living with them pleasantly. These desires are invariant characteris-tics. In fact, to fulfill these desires students are often willing to make sacrifices. In a recent survey at a large state university, students were asked whether they would continue going to college if they knew positively that in the future they would be no better off financially than if they had not gone. More than three-fourths (83 percent) answered in the affirmative. When asked whether they would have gone to college if they knew positively they would be making *less* money than if they had not gone to college, nearly half bravely still said yes.

These responses recall what Suzanne Langer, in *Philosophy in a New Key*, said about art: it is far from being casual play, but most societies, "primitive" and other, are willing to accept often excruciating pain and effort in its pursuit. Making sense of the world and finding meaning in life are perhaps the primary human desires, and these desires are to be expected in college students as well. But somehow administrators, not unlike many parents, assume a pragmatism in students that in fact is not nearly as overgrown as they think. In some ways, adults' concern about jobs has created a rhetoric with which students comply. By regarding job preparation as so exclusively central to a college education, the elders curtail the students' imagination and, thus, their possibilities.

A hard-headed administrator might go only by the enrollment figures, which show that students are flocking to the pragmatic subjects—business, health sciences, engineering, accounting. But this is precisely the point at which knowledgeable leadership comes in. Often the value of "pragmatic" undergraduate courses in the labor market is exaggerated. The requisite training often is best received on the job. The pragmatic choices often are hurried, requiring later shifts in education and training. Some institutions have hit on the imaginative solution of offering business minors, computer minors, and the like, leaving students room to pursue other interests in their major.

But the job of leadership, above all, is to enlist faculty and other staff members in the task of helping students become aware of their deeper motivations for making sense of their lives and their world, to relieve their anxieties about pursuing an *educational* course in college, and to develop the structures and programs that will allow them simultaneously to prepare for the marketplace and to cultivate their intellect and sensitivities. Many young people have, economically speaking, become nonfunctional (a fact institutions may not have wholly accepted), and institutions may be seeking economic justifications for this age group that American society cannot accommodate. A college or university president should be able to provide leadership that moves the institution beyond enslavement to the false dichotomy of vocational education versus liberal education.

Many other factors have contributed to the "watering down" of education. Perhaps the one most frequently cited is the influx of many kinds of students who previously did not attend college. This assertion can provoke endless arguments about whether there is a limited talent pool, but these arguments are ultimately an evasion of the task: to set expectations and standards that elicit good work from students *in the context of their own lives*. As the president of a large municipal institution remarked:

> Here we are in an age in which the information that is available to us has increased almost a hundredfold and is increasing twenty times each year. We are living in a highly technological age, and we're still frightened of it. People insist on forcing our kind of college into a mold. They suggest that if we change the color of our institution, the racial mix, or the age of the students, the purity of our academic program is endangered. I resent that suggestion; it disturbs me. The 45-year-old woman who could not get an education when she was 18 or 21 is a precious entity, her mind is a precious entity, as is the black student from the ghetto, as is the Puerto Rican from the Bronx, as is the Indian from wherever, as is the Pakistani. Unless someone recognizes that these people can be brought together and liberally educated, higher education will go down the tube.

Other factors that contribute to the watering down of education are the higher student-to-faculty ratios and the tendency of many faculty members to spend less time on teaching and more on other pursuits—that is, giving in to the pressure of performing for their peers for the sake of recognition, money, and job security. For the involved teacher, the teacher willing to experiment in ways of presenting a subject, "underprepared" or "unmotivated" students do not exist. The universal search for meaning and knowledge is a powerful incentive to get nearly every student involved. Lack of imagination is often more pronounced in a teacher than in a student, and often there are no structures and incentives to encourage teachers to deviate from the routine.

Head hunting and hucksterism can predominate over education leadership because of an institution's economic needs and its conformity to prevailing economic attitudes. The central idea of some academic advertising is to make people buy the product, regardless of whether it is particularly suitable for them. This kind of advertising smacks of travel brochures that stress the importance of, for example, visiting London and seeing the Tower and Westminster Cathedral, regardless of whether the experience fits in with the person's life or enriches it. The degree counts, and the courses may be largely forgotten. Perhaps a business cannot be expected to close shop because the merchandise is shabby, but an education institution may be expected to try to educate in ways that make sense. If it cannot attract the students for that purpose, it might decide it has no further reason for existence.

Discussion about concern for student development in the 1980s has a quaint ring to it. Students went out of fashion, in a manner of speaking, in the fall of 1970. When they stopped protesting, they could be neglected. What institutions reaped from this attitude was a decade of relative passivity, during which students' interest in focusing their minds and passions on the nature of their education and the nature of society slackened. American society was thus left bereft of some good ideas, and students were left bereft of opportunities to develop skills for independent thinking and effective social and political participation. In many classrooms today, faculty members confront reluctant, passive students, some of them lost to apathy, alcohol, drugs, and occasional destructiveness, such as vandalism. The net loss to the academy and to society is the loss of zest, imagination, constructive reform, and productivity.

One need not be a particularly astute prophet to say that student protest is not just a phenonmenon of the past. The same conditions that gave rise to it before will give rise to it again. For example, in 1980 three-fourths of the entering freshmen nationwide declared that students should help evaluate faculty members. The conditions that once generated protest are founded in institutions that are insufficiently responsive to the expressive, creative, and meaning-seeking propensities of the young. Forward-looking presidents might mentally prepare themselves for the next round of protest.

More important for the present, presidents would be well advised to provide for their students opportunities for enlarged expression in thought, art, and action, and for participation in the smaller society of the campus and the larger society around it. Through such actions and activities students can sharpen their minds and their human and social capacities. This goal of enlarged expression might be the first item on the agenda of the education-minded president.

These last remarks have focused not only on what presidents need to know, but also on what they need to *do*. They need to involve students in the educational and administrative process. If students currently are often passive on committees, this behavior should be understood as a symptom, a perception of pointlessness, rather than an expression of disinterest. The president might see to it that, department by department, students are called on to assist, in appropriate ways, in planning, executing, and evaluating course offerings. The president should also encourage student participation with regard to planning and coordinating various student services, residential life, and the life of commuting students while on campus (special attention will also enable commuters to shape their off-campus lives in more educational and developmental ways).

The president's communication with students has already been discussed. When given the opportunity, students can develop an almost statesmanlike understanding of the functioning of the presidency. Our interviews furnish many examples of student statesmanship. One student referred to his president's behavior in committees as one of "constructive ambiguity." He goes on to say,

> This phrase perhaps sums up his role in those deliberations, possibly even in the college. Caught as he is between a need to formulate consensus with the people who pay the bills, the students, and the board of managers, he sees his role as one of constructive ambiguity. He will sit around in a meeting for an hour or two waiting for some compromise to develop and then step into it with sense and deliberation and always caution. He does this well; but I don't think this is the time for that kind of leadership. At a time when people are confused, it's nice to know where some people stand.

Often students' views of the institution are much less limited than those of faculty members. This difference in perspective is not surprising, for like the president, students can view the institution as a whole and not, as in the case of faculty members, from the vantage point of special interests. This kind of talent needs to be harnessed— for the sake of the institution and for the sake of the individual student. It cannot be stressed enough that increased contacts with students would greatly humanize the president's job and make it more enjoyable.

The bibliography at the end of this chapter lists several books that a president should read to learn about student development. These provide a variety of perspectives on the student experience. The annotated bibliography by Sally S. Gaff and associates can steer presidents further.

Government and Higher Education

The image of the college president as the executive who, of all chief executives, is most free from government entanglement is a part of higher education folklore that dies hard. Since the founding of Harvard in 1636, the presiding officer—college president, presiding professor, board of overseers, or whoever the presiding officer might be—has lived a routine of such accountings and regulation compliances as has been required of a chartered corporation by state, federal, and, to an extent not often realized, local civil authority.

In the past 350 years, the relationship between higher education and the federal government has grown increasingly complicated. Most of the complications have come from the impetus of at least five high points of federal initiative: the Morrill Land Grant Act of 1862 and its successors; Public Law 346, commonly known as the G.I. Bill of Rights of 1944; the National Defense Education Act of 1958; the Higher Education Act of 1965; and the Education Amendments of 1972, which, by means of the Basic Education Opportunity Grant (now called Pell Grants), declared higher education to be a citizen's right not to be denied by lack of economic means.

These acts will almost certainly not be the last in the line of government linchpin actions to secure equal education opportunity nationwide. The country's commitment to higher education access has made student financial aid in its many forms a required course for college and university executives; each year it becomes more pertinent to planning the operating budget.[9]

Details like these portray U.S. higher education, despite its intentions to be diverse and free from regimentation, as more and more like an immense network of instruction centers, each constrained by the reality that it costs more to educate twelve million Americans than any combination of sources can make possible without supplementary federal aid. Particularly hard hit are the 1,660 private institutions, only a handful of which have officially declared a policy of nonacceptance of federal or state funds; colleges such as Rockford, Hillsdale, and Wabash are examples.

Government involvement has kept pace with the growth in the number and size of institutions, particularly state colleges and universities, and one reverse effect has been a proliferation of subsystems within states. These subsystems are not consolidated and, therefore, continually compete for legislative appropriations. A public university president who was interviewed noted the effect: "Five different representations—that is, one from each of the five public institutions, with no real coordination among them—are made to the legislators for funds." This particular situation has since been corrected by centralized reorganization. In numerous states, however, subsystems of public institutions, reporting to separate boards of control, continue to vie for appropriations. In contrast, private institutions have formu-

9. See Elaine El-Khawas, *Special Policy Issues in Management of Student Aid* (Washington, D.C.: American Council on Education, 1980).

lated a unified approach for achieving tuition grants, contract arrangements, and occasional direct cost-of-education subsidies.

Rising costs and enrollment competition point to continuing activity by federal and state governments in regulating institutional finances. Since 1960, the costs of accounting and reporting have become a major part of administrative expenditures. Decades ago, college presidents were wise to foster relations with the institution's affiliated church, so that they might honestly claim innocence of involvement with state government. For all but strictly sectarian schools, that day is gone. State aid of one kind or another, whether for a public or a private college, is a fact of life demanding constant administrative attention. The sectarian schools, meanwhile, have significantly changed their forms of governance so as to supersede ineligibility for public grants because of the First Amendment. The so-called Bundy Bill of 1968 in New York State resulted in a special legislative commission for the purpose of ruling on whether a given college could be declared sufficiently free from church control to receive Bundy funds as an independent institution.

The years following World War II saw a long period of growth for higher education, during which time the federal government, under circumstances that have already been mentioned, became a strong supporter of higher education. During the same period there was a steady increase in laws and regulations affecting institutions, as well as moves to enforce compliance. This trend, which has accelerated during the past ten years, concurs with a decline in predicted future enrollment and an increase in financial stress on institutions.

Colleges and universities now routinely retain lawyers and special administrators to deal with federal agents regarding affirmative action and financial accountability for research and program grants. A struggle has formed around the question, How much authority does the federal government have to tell higher education what to do? Brigham Young, a large well-funded, church-affiliated university, came to the breaking point with the federal government and announced simply that its own governing principles precluded further compliance with federal rulings on affirmative action.

As adversarial positions stiffened, the Alfred P. Sloan Foundation acted to resolve differences by creating in February 1977 the Sloan Commission on the Regulation of Higher Education. The commission took two years to address the following issues: (1) How does the country strike a balance between institutional freedom and government authority? (2) To what extent is the academic institution to be responsive to what may be perceived as social needs? The commission determined that both the regulators and the regulated need a detailed, comprehensive analysis of the regulatory process by a distinguished but disinterested body whose recommendations would define and protect—and be seen to define and protect—the public interest. The Sloan Commission's findings were summarized by Carl Kaysen, executive director of the Annual Meeting of the American Council on Education in November 1979. The complete report was published the next year.

The most useful lesson of the Sloan Commission report is that it illustrates how government involvement increases with the cost of the enterprise and how it points inexorably toward greater central control. A stated objective of the Sloan study was to propose means of moving toward greater institutional freedom from federal government. The alternative that seems to have emerged is greater state control.

Two of the report's proposals have caused concern among college educators. One proposal suggests that the state government should evaluate, certify, and decertify education programs in each public college and university, while *inviting* private institutions to participate in the state evaluation programs. The second proposal advocates that voluntary regional accreditation be enhanced through visits by representatives of outside peer institutions but that the regional evaluations be considered as advisory to the state involved and not in themselves decisive. The latter proposal reflects the strongest advocacy made by any national commission in recent years toward greater state control of college and university operations and away from nongovernment voluntary accreditation. Voluntary accreditation by regional commissions during most of the twentieth century has been accepted as the basis for eligibility to receive federal and state funding and as a general indication of quality.

The foregoing illustration of government activity in evaluation and control raises the perennial question of what political know-how a prospective college president should have. In Aristotle's view, the question is redundant, since man by nature is a political animal. Any distinctions, therefore, between the politics of organized government and the day-to-day activities of directing the activities of any organization, private or public, become matters of circumstance rather than differences in kind, so far as the leader's actions are concerned.

Nonetheless, the costs of education give the matter of government aid increasing weight in planning the college's budget and plant. As a result, a college president's influence in Washington and in the respective state houses (not to mention with leading state representatives scattered throughout the region) is becoming an increasingly important requisite of presidential effectiveness. However, how the president's political acumen can be best employed is still dependent, happily, on a diversity of human talents. A president can lead his or her cause politically in any number of ways—from outright charisma to a quiet integrity effectively expressed. (The late Harold Dodds of Princeton was a master of the latter style.)

One thing is reasonably certain: consumerism in higher education is here to stay. Responding to it properly—that is, avoiding errors such as slipping into commercialism—is a skill that should become part of each president's tool kit of effective human relations skills. Along with consumerism comes an equal stress on the ability to explain to public policy makers what the particular educational strength of a college or university best prepares it to do. The political setting may require a president to face openly the issue of whether his or her institution's program is geared to the needs of its immediate environment.

When this issue was raised at the University of Wisconsin at Green Bay, it prompted the question of whether the major academic rationale on which this branch campus had been founded in 1965— environmental and international studies—was appropriate to the region and should be continued. Opinion of the surrounding lay public favored more emphasis on business and engineering courses. At times like these, local politics can easily influence events in the state capitol, and issues of broad education versus practical training—i.e., issues with far-reaching financial implications—may be sharply drawn.

Visits to both small private institutions and large public institutions strengthened our impression, similar to the Sloan Commission's prognosis, that American higher education can look forward to continuing government involvement. As a result of the prevailing climate of potentially fewer students and higher unit costs, the adjective *independent*, when applied to college operations, more closely describes basic academic freedom than the processes of planning and program and budget control. Government relations, whether state or federal, have a prominent place on every campus. Fiscal accountability to the public will increase as the number of students paying full tuition decreases and as government aids such as the Pell Grants become more important items in institutional planning. The cumulative poise of the intellectual independence of strong universities during past centuries will be required of presidents who wish to lead their faculties in living with the consequences of such statements as this: "Program review needs to be developed through the participation of institutions and their faculty *and of the statewide higher education agency and with the cooperative reinforcement of the legislative and executive branches of state government.*" [italics added][10] To many educators, "program review" is the Education Commission of the State's euphemism for the issue of freedom to teach what the college wants to and is able to teach.

The prospect of increased government intervention in higher education is seldom discussed in search committee interviews with presidential candidates. However, it does pose another set of criteria to be included in the screening process. The decades since World War II have seen a rise in number of college presidents who come from posts in the federal government, particularly the State Department and its foreign service staff. (Presidents from career service in the military continue to be few.) Yet inasmuch as the majority of chief administrators still come from the faculty or from academic administration, political rapport with government agents will remain a talent to be borrowed from experience in institutional politics. Dealing with government representatives, as many presidents indicate in their more candid writings about the politics affecting their job, may actually require few new skills.

Some state political problems concerning higher education are too thorny for even the most polished, most politically minded president to handle. Many of these problems deal with unresolved social dilemmas that constantly recur. Equal access to college versus meritocracy, the tensions between academic freedom and public accountability, and the professionalization of intercollegiate athletics are three hardy perennials that will stay with us as surely as death and taxes. In areas like these, the leader of the institution can best demonstrate political savoir faire by maintaining a delicate balance between his or her reasoned conclusions and the necessity to live with the potency of nonrational belief.

Economic Prospects for Colleges and Universities

One of the most effective ways to discourage capable potential candidates from seriously considering a college presidency is to forecast a career shackled to keeping the organization afloat: "You don't want to spend your whole time raising money, do you?" Such

10. *Challenge, Coordination, and Governance,* p. xv.

wet-blanket approaches come from the undeniable fact that elee-mosynary institutions have had a harder time of it in the 1970s than in the '50s and '60s, particularly since the 1974 recession and the OPEC oil price explosion. Public colleges, likewise, have had to adjust to shrinking appropriations on a constant-dollar basis as state and federal funding policy has tightened. During the 1970s, federal and state moneys awarded to higher education reflected a deliberate trend away from grants to institutions and toward per-student formulas. The broadening of access for young persons was the prime objective, and the result was a heavier emphasis on enrollment growth. Since tuition pays only part of the cost of higher education, the change sharpened the need for additional funds from other sources.

In *The Costs of Higher Education* (1980), Howard Bowen focuses on fundamental questions about how much money is needed to provide an adequate college education for the individual student. Bowen has consistently held that an institution's need has no measurable top—i.e., an institution can spend any amount of money it can acquire and still be able to demonstrate a need for more in order to keep improving educational quality. Restating his long-held position, he produces evidence that at least one-fifth of American colleges and universities spend less than an acceptable amount of funds per student: "The overwhelming problem for much of American higher education is not inefficiency or waste but sheer undernourishment."[11] At the same time, Bowen emphasizes that many colleges with modest resources have managed to accomplish significant intellectual and personal growth in students. These institutions may in fact justify their efforts better than some colleges whose reputation and academic strength have attracted students who are better prepared and who show less relative growth in four years than do students in less affluent schools.

Waste occurs in higher education as in all organizations. In the leaner decade of the 1970s, institutions of higher education trimmed waste and also sustained losses in program features that make for quality. The present decade appears to be one of declining enrollment. If colleges and universities are to hold on to their support sources, they must improve their study of outcomes. With better understanding of how to measure the yield of a college education, colleges and universities can put themselves in better position to ask for a leveling of support (for example, through block grants not tied precisely to

11. Howard Bowen, *The Costs of Higher Education* (San Francisco: Jossey-Bass, 1980), p. 245.

enrollment count) so that quality performance may improve even though the size of the student body decreases.

Selling that concept to legislators and donors does not entirely answer the opening claim that presidents exist mainly to beg for dollars. Still, the quality of an institution and its leadership can be gauged in other ways. No one can say exactly how much money a college needs to be excellent. But Bowen reminds us that good education depends on other products of leadership—"intangible qualities such as clarity of purpose, dedication, sense of community, love of learning and teaching, personal interest in students, and prudent administration."[12]

Most people who study colleges closely will agree with Bowen and other observers that the difference in quality outcomes between rich and not-rich institutions has many exceptions—too many, in fact, to justify a prospective candidate's rejecting the offer of a college presidency solely because the institution is not one of the financially elite. The bulk of America's 3,000 institutions stands on the middle ground between wealth and impoverishment. The existence of these middle-ground institutions, as the Carnegie Council pointed out in its 1980 report, is not guaranteed during the two decades ahead. On the other hand, less than 4 percent of these institutions have closed in the past decade, a figure that represents better odds of survival than does the record of most other kinds of organizations.

The heavy emphasis on management skills and systems in the college presidency is a result of the past fifteen years of growth, changing clientele, and increasingly complex interrelations with government at all levels. These trends have persuaded numerous writers on higher education that the successful president of the future will closely resemble the heads of other complex organizations; he or she will have good management and decision-making skills and will delegate education functions to second-level specialists, such as a provost or vice president for academic administration. Yet testimony from various institutions reported in the previous chapters reveals little acceptance of the concept of the manager-president, even though management was clearly in evidence, especially in the multicampus university presidencies.

It can be predicted with fair certainty that college and university constituencies in the future will take for granted that the president has the necessary managerial knowledge and follow-through. In addition

12. Ibid., p. 229.

to good management skills, the president must also have skills in human relationships and an understanding of educational purpose, skills that will not be taken for granted. Most important, perhaps, will be a willingness to stand by certain values embodied by a particular college or university, values that the new president should help reidentify. Value priorities often become lost, buried in the avalanche of daily procedure. If the new president shows abilities like these, his or her tenure may not only survive financial challenge but may provide the kind of leadership that makes lasting differences in the life of the institution.

Obviously, predictions about the future college president should not be based on theories that human nature, in or out of the executive setting, will materially change. Men and women who have been appointed to positions of power will continue to react, first, according to the kind of persons they are and, second, according to the setting in which they exercise their leadership.

The data of the Presidency Project confirmed our assumption that college presidents are substantially the same. They also confirmed the reality of executive power and its impact on decision making in even the strongest, most faculty-oriented institutions. That reality affects two main areas of the organization: (1) the faculty corporation and (2) the president's administrative structure. In a few universities, student leadership is strong enough to provide a third area of constituent reaction to presidential power.

The nature of faculty participation in campus governance varies by institution, as it does by department, committee and, indeed, by individuals. Governance on campus ranges from perfunctory consultation with the administrative hierarchy to lengthy, controversial and—too seldom—well-knit councils of faculty members, administrators, and students that make genuinely collective decisions on school policy.

The central administration may range from quasi-military line-and-staff organization or Weberian bureaucracy to a freely structured group around the president that takes on varying assignments according to priorities. The more adaptive administrative stance reflects the fluidity of institutional circumstances that first became evident in the mid-1960s. Few institutions are so firmly established in their settings as to have missed this experience. Harvard and Columbia survived, while other institutions—such as Franconia College and Windham College—ceased operating.

Incoming presidents know from talking with incumbents that adaptive leadership has become the test of durability (not to mention forward movement) of the contemporary college. Changes in the college and university setting noted in this chapter have included the increase in the number of campuses linked in systems (as opposed to free-standing); the growing tendency of faculties to be centered by discipline throughout the system rather than united in a single campus; increased attention, generated by students, to the need for an educational process continuous with their life concerns and with the world environment; the more direct entry of government, both federal and state, into the planning, programming, budget control, and evaluation of private as well as public institutions; and the inexorable pressures for business management and systems efficiency that have come from government involvement in particular and from rising costs of operating a labor-intensive organization in general.

Facing these and other changes, such as faculty unionization, the future president might easily succumb to a corporate management model, as some indeed have done. Our own survey shows that most presidents, faculty members, and students prefer that the head of the college be an educator. In view of the heavy managerial priorities of presidents' schedules as well as the predominant opinions among those interviewed that incumbent presidents reflected management rather than education leadership, the seriousness of the preference is doubtful. Still, nearly a third of the presidents were viewed by their constituents as being educators, at least by the president's own values, if not by the events of a typical president's day.

The president's value structure, insofar as it is known, counts heavily with his or her campus community. For faculty members, the president's values are revealed by the consistency of his or her work for academic program support or by a clear stand on institutional purpose before the public, particularly the alumni and the legislature. For students, the president's values were seen in the stands he or she took on their behalf—for example, listening to them about matters important to them, such as innovative programs, quality of teaching, examinations, and so forth—even when the eventual decision went against them. For the academic community as a whole, the president's value structure comes to light on some issues of social justice where material and humane considerations are at odds with each other, such as Kingman Brewster's celebrated comments on a minority person's chance for fair trial in New Haven. Although such issues have faded since the 1960s, the sentiments remain unchanged.

The successful college president of the future will need to show enough managerial wisdom to conduct the institution through increasing government scrutiny as financial burdens increase and as student constituencies become more heterogeneous. Most alumni will continue to resist change except for the rise in their college's prestige as reflected in opinions of their associates or in the mass media.

Human issues will present the subtler tests of leadership. A president may, by tapping the sources of wealth and maintaining political approval, be able to keep an institution afloat. More important, he or she must be a person of sensitivity to individuals.

Bibliography on Student Development

Astin, Alexander W. *Four Critical Years: Effects of College on Beliefs, Attitudes, and Knowledge.* San Francisco: Jossey-Bass, 1978.

Bowen, Howard R. *Investment in Learning: The Individual and Social Value of American Higher Education.* San Francisco: Jossey-Bass, 1977.

Chickering, Arthur. *The Modern American College.* San Francisco: Jossey-Bass, 1981.

Erikson, Erik. *Identity and the Life Cycle: Selected Papers.* Psychological Issues Monograph, no. 1, vol. 1. New York: International Universities Press, 1967.

Feldman, Kenneth A., and Newcomb, Theodore M. *The Impact of College on Students.* San Francisco: Jossey-Bass, 1969.

Gaff, Sally S., et al. *Professional Development: A Guide to Resources.* New Rochelle, N. Y.: Change Magazine Press, 1978.

Hazen Foundation. *The Student in Higher Education.* New Haven, Conn., 1968.

Katz, Joseph, et al. *No Time for Youth: Growth and Constraint in College Students.* San Francisco: Jossey-Bass, 1968.

Perry, William G. *Forms of Intellectual and Ethical Development in the College Years.* New York: Holt, Rinehart, and Winston, 1970.

Raushenbush, Esther. *The Student and His Studies.* Middletown, Conn.: Wesleyan University Press, 1964.

Sanford, Nevitt. *The American College.* New York: Wiley, 1962.

White, Robert W. *Lives in Progress.* 3rd ed. New York: Holt, Rinehart, and Winston, 1975.

6 Learning Presidential Leadership

The leader of any modern organization plays out his or her role in the ghostly light of past eras when leadership was something into which one person among thousands was born. A person born to leadership might become a good leader or a bad one or one who steadily improved; history is replete with stories of kings who learned from their mistakes. Yet leadership by divine right, an idea that most cultures discarded about the time of the invention of gunpowder, still remains the prevailing concept of a few theocratic societies of the Eastern world. If the leader is not born in the palace to the royal family, he may be sought out by appointed messengers acting under divine guidance, much as the Wise Men followed the star to Bethlehem.

This analogy may seem far removed from the current procedures of selecting the chief executive officer of an American college. The choice, or acceptance, of the head of a theocracy can be traced, however faintly, to leadership by divine right. This ancient concept reflects in part the American colonials' decision to found colleges on the ecclesiastical models of Oxford and Cambridge. The church hierarchy was not known for its democratic approach in matters of appointment. Seniority was a more important prerequisite than judgment of fitness to head an order or a college; social status remained most important of all. As for leadership, decisions on curriculum were prescribed by tradition. The only issues involving some choice might include which of the medieval scholars were held most in favor or how far the spirit of the Renaissance, with its revival of Greek and Latin (i.e., pagan) writers, should be permitted to invade the dominance of Aquinas or Augustine.

Until after the Civil War, American college presidents came almost exclusively from the clergy, as did professors. Not until the land-grant movement had introduced agriculture and engineering into the curriculum and the German concept of graduate specialization had been imported from abroad did matters of curricular choice, made famous in the late 1860s by Eliot of Harvard, give content to academic administration.

After each of the two World Wars, college enrollment expanded and diversified. Students were older, faculties more independent and specialized. Experimental curricula replaced Eliot's notion of free election and the various systems of majors and minors that followed him. More genuine attempts were made at student-oriented programs of study, as Frederick Rudolph has traced in *Curriculum: A History of the American Undergraduate Course of Study Since 1636* (1977). Decisions about what to study and how to prepare for a growing number of professions focused attention on college planning and direction by officers who by now did more than keep attendance records or discipline lagging students.

Campus resident life, meanwhile, passed through the long decades of church-dominated regulation and became a more secularized society, much like that of the world outside. World War II veterans who returned to college chipped away at the concept of in loco parentis; the job was finished by the student movements of the late 1960s. (Truthfully, college administrators were ready to be relieved of the duty.) Financial factors, meanwhile, added manifoldly to the task of managing a complicated order of assignments, a task necessary for guiding a modern institution of learning.

Higher education has a history of moving toward faculty and student interdependence. Despite this movement, however, the data from our campus study leave no room for doubting either the growth of a technology of management or the contemporary college's need for such organization. As is the case with other social organizations, a college's accomplishments—in fact, the very ambiance of a campus—quickly revealed to the perceptive visitor the nature of leadership at the top. No amount of diplomacy on the part of those interviewed could conceal collective judgments about how satisfactorily the institution was being led.

The popular heresy that colleges actually run as well or better when the president is away was not seriously advanced. In the main, the statement heard more often than any others was this: "The president is away a great deal. We know he has to be out raising money, but things might go better at the college if he gave the institution more time." The ACE-UCLA Freshman National Norms, published each fall, do not list "Would like to see more of the president and know him as a person" as a prominent student attitude. In this case, the respondents were all freshmen, and freshmen are not usually concerned about the president's role. In our own discussions, on the other hand, the president's attention to the college community figured plainly in our talks with faculty members, students, and fellow administrators.

When those interviewed conceded that the president was a desirable campus fixture, it was natural to ask how his or her presence helped make things go better. The answers can be roughly summarized as, "The president knows a lot about this place. He (or she) is the one who really knows what's going on because he (or she) is the one who has to make most of the decisions. Students and faculty want to be in on the decision-making process, but everyone knows the president has the final say in most matters."

Does the president's ability to act well and wisely, then, make for institutional progress? If so, how can these qualities best be brought to light? Are there books that instruct presidents how to improve their performance?

The surest way to prepare a president for excellent service is to select an excellent president to begin with. The quality of an appointed candidate and his or her subsequent performance in the executive post are closely intertwined. Thus, the first step in learning about presidential leadership is to learn about the process of the presidential search.

A spate of recent articles centers on the executive search problem: *Fortune* featured an article on head hunters (October 1979), and the *New York Times Magazine* carried the rather disturbing article "Why Big Business Is Firing the Boss" (March 8, 1981). The business world, having gone overboard for professional executive search firms, now feels both confident and anxious about the prospect of quick turnover in senior management. Contracts are written for six-figure contracts, with carry-over clauses in case of early separations as well as various bonuses and options. So long as the head-hunting firm is able to attract a successor whom the firm agrees once again to cushion against personal financial disaster, corporations feel protected against being without top executives for an extended period of time.

But what about the morale of the rest of the staff? In a company producing so many units of automotive equipment per day, morale may or may not be of crying concern. In an institution of learning, the interpersonal dynamics are different. To have the president walk in and out of the job within a year, then to see the process repeated six months later, is bound to affect persons who are trying to persuade human beings of certain values of organized collegiate study. The chief executive of an industrial organization may enter and leave the position via a revolving door, but the university ostensibly stands for a certain permanency in human affairs.

Trustees have been slow to see the differences between their function as college stewards and the function of corporation directors. Much of the trouble starts with the trustees' failure to sit with faculty members, administrators, and students long enough to gain an understanding of the sensitiveness of the interaction among departments and schools in a center of higher learning. All constituencies are impelled to learn, difficult as it may be, to judge presidents on their interpersonal skills. For example, the questions serious presidential candidates ask about whom, how, and what the institution has decided to teach indicate more about how they will wear with the faculty than do their appearance, field accomplishments, or the names of the organizations they have previously served.

John Nason's *Presidential Search* reviews records of 326 presidential search committees. Some of the governing boards were advisory (as in the SUNY system) and included no trustees. However, when the time comes to elect the chief executive, the trustees are fully in place as the court of decision.

Here, in fact, is the hint of a rather serious slip. The evaluation of a candidate as thinker and educator takes place at the committee level or in small faculty and student interviews arranged by the committee. Is the candidate attuned to this particular job? Is he or she familiar with the teaching process at this institution, the evaluation of learning, the tenure and promotion wrangles, the treatment of minority and women appointments—in short, the chief elements that make up the business of administering this particular college? The faculty can expose the candidate to all these issues. Typically, however, this kind of information does not filter through to the board, even though other accomplishments (including, perhaps, a record quarter-mile race won thirty years ago) will be recorded on page after page.

The road to excellence in the college presidency is best traveled by someone who has been in similar terrain before. Whether the road was large and impressive, filled with important travelers, or narrow and rutted with only light traffic, is less significant than that the grade was similar.

Specifically, institutions do amazingly little as yet to discover how much exposure the prospective president has had to such subjects as department budgets, the source of large gifts or grants for different purposes, the mix of academic divisions and their dangers, the meaning of the humanities, the dynamics of the youth generation, the religious concerns of students, and sexuality and family problems. If a prospective industrial C.E.O. were not evaluated in a similar way in regard to employee relations in a union shop, civil service employment comparisons, federal government confrontation, personnel relations at the second and third plant levels, production schedules, line versus staff duties, foreign competition in the company's products, and so on, the executive search team would, or should, soon be out of business. Yet every month presidents of colleges and major universities are elected with scarcely a mention of issues that are pertinent to the problems they will encounter every day in the executive chair and the meeting halls.

The answer to the first question of selecting a president, then, is, Study your college or university until not only the committee but also the full board are aware of the institution's peculiar characteristics as well as its general nature. Then reduce the list of prospects (it is common to boast of "four hundred candidates," which, under today's sunshine laws, means exactly nothing) to a small few who can converse with interest, humor, and some specific knowledge about what the college asks its president, as its leader, to do daily.

Most presidents learn to exploit the merits they bring to the office. Whether a candidate can learn to improve his or her leadership at this particular institution is the final question to be considered. If the committee and the board have prepared the way by locating the person whose experience is most closely geared to the specific actions required in the job, the institution will have taken a step toward ensuring that the right actions will be taken and that the performance will steadily improve.

Conventional Routes to the College Presidency Today

The next question that should be considered is, What amount of training can go on before or after a candidate has been selected president? Of the twenty-five presidents interviewed in the Presidency Project, twenty have their Ph.D.'s, one an Ed.D., and one an M.D. Three have no doctoral degrees. Most of the Ph.D.'s were earned in academic disciplines, but one was in administration. At least twenty of the presidents had taught at the college or university level, and twenty-one had been college administrators before becoming president. Twelve had also served as administrators, scientists, or attorneys in federal bureaus, municipal government, or higher education agencies. One had been a journalist, one a business executive, and another a member of a religious order.

Although a few of the presidents had moved from a teaching position to an administrative post within the same institution, most went on to the presidency of another institution. Only one moved directly from the faculty to the presidency of the same institution; another had previously taught at the institution she now headed but came directly from an administrative post there.

To judge from the Presidency Project data, training for leadership of a college most often consists of working one's way up the administrative line—in most cases, the academic administrative line—after previous experience as a professor.[1] Most presidents tend to come from within the organizational structure of a college. In such cases, the only gap to be crossed is that from professor—often, though by no means always, a department chairperson—to full-time administrator.

At the present time an increasing minority of presidents come from the field of public affairs—for example, from the diplomatic service, other federal bureaus, and various independent or public agencies serving higher education. Presidents from the military are not uncommon, especially in the South; in most regions, however, their tenures are neither long nor especially notable.

Etzioni's contrast between line organization and rank organization, mentioned previously, holds true: military officers, because of their long habit of assuming obedience to superior command, often have difficulty handling the persistent tendency to challenge authority that goes deep in the academician. On their own grounds of knowledge and teaching, faculty members do not relinquish their peerage. Undoubtedly, the shining exception of presidential leadership by a former general was Robert E. Lee at Washington College (later Washington and Lee University). Yet his distinguished academic career occurred a century ago, when hierarchical authority in a college was accepted by students and faculty members to a degree not customary today.

The largest number of nonacademics (using the term in the strict sense) who assume presidencies come from the law profession. According to a popular view, this development is a reaction to increasingly litigious trends in institutional affairs. However, almost no presidents come into office directly from law practice, unless, for example, they were trustees pressed into an acting presidency, per-

1. See also Frederick deW. Bolman, *How College Presidents Are Chosen* (Washington, D.C.: American Council on Education, 1965).

haps after a sudden departure by the incumbent. More commonly, lawyer presidents have previously served as law school deans or have held comparable administrative posts in other organizations. In these cases, the training for leadership is much like that of an academic dean, provost, vice president for finance, or dean of students—the most common stepping stones, as has been mentioned. Given the overproduction of law graduates today, the trend bids fair to continue.

Presidential Training — Systematic or on the Job?

Officers chosen for military command schools may be said to have been already tapped as potential four-star officers. In contrast, training for the college presidency, not to mention a major university presidency, is so sparse and unsystematic that it can hardly be said to exist in a formal sense. Universities here and there have offered doctoral degree programs in what has been labeled college administration; Teachers College of Columbia University, for example, dates its program in college administration back nearly fifty years. A few aspiring administrators become Ph.D. candidates in political science or public administration but select a topic in higher education for their dissertation.

It soon became evident, however, that whatever else might eventually come to the person with a doctorate in college administration, a college presidency was least likely. In the academic world, antipedagogy biases are strong. Universities offering college administration sequences—such as Stanford, New York University, and others—found the wiser approach was to offer a broad program in higher education and to fit the degree holder with some specialty within the field. After World War II, research and data rapidly accumulated in several areas of higher education study. There are now several hundred professors of higher education in the country. As is the case with academicians in other specialties, most of them have turned down or have not yet been invited to take administrative posts.

The multiple challenges, not to say pitfalls, inherent in the job of the college president have long been recognized, but the question persists: Why aren't people trained for leadership of a college? This question is reinforced by comments about the number of highly intelligent and sensitive persons in a college community whose careers are directly affected by the quality of the president's performance. In particular, the president should be aware that personal problems sometimes affect staff members' performance. Too often these problems are hastily or insensitively handled because of the daily press of the executive schedule. Good presidents are not born, yet neither are they made—at least not in the sense of being directly trained. The best of them learn social and decision-making skills early in life, and then learn to apply these skills after their tour of duty as president has begun.

The idea of a community of peers, which has undergirded most of this discussion, lives on among academicians, along with the notion that training a man or woman to serve as a professor's boss is demeaning in a profession of peers. Granted, as our data have repeatedly shown, most faculty members want a president who strongly upholds the institution. But many faculty members also believe that this strength should be equated with the president's readiness to concede leadership to them in areas of education policy, where their experience qualifies them to act as a court of opinion, if not to lead in decision making. How to balance executive strength with forbearance is not an easy subject to teach. It may, perhaps, be learned, provided the president can absorb the realities of the local situation, but not from a textbook on faculty psychology—or so reasons the academic mind. The education of the philosopher-king is, even among Platonists, still classified as a utopian ideal. Machiavelli's *The Prince* is more likely to be popularly identified as the training manual of college presidents.

Today, in fact, there are numerous leadership training programs based on a view of higher education as a broad field of skilled service. Since college administration has followed other complex organizations into group management, the training can be addressed in general terms of application to management situations and need no longer be specified as a course geared to the presidency. Academic affairs, student affairs, finance and business, research administration, admissions and counseling, and public relations and development are generally the core elements of management units in any institution with more than 1,500 students; larger institutions may have many more management units.

Starting in 1961, The Ellis L. Phillips Foundation inaugurated a small program of selected young academicians whose interests and aptitudes inclined them toward college administration in any of several management fields. Aided by the Ford Foundation and the Hazen Foundation, the program grew until it was transferred to the American Council on Education. Under the new name of the ACE Fellows Program, it was expanded to include an average of forty

Fellows per year. It continues today on a self-funding basis; the host institutions carry the costs of the program. The records show that seventy of the 650 ACE Fellows since 1965 have become presidents. Four hundred others have found posts at the level of provost, vice president, or dean. Many have returned to teaching; others have left higher education for employment elsewhere. The program is low-key and has, by and large, become accepted in the academic profession. If it had been conducted explicitly as a school for future presidents, it might have fared differently.

The ACE Fellows Program, supervised by an officer in Washington but otherwise left much to the direction of the individual participating institutions, consists typically of assigning the Fellow to the president, academic vice president, dean of student affairs, or, sometimes, head financial officer. As for any administrator, the duties vary from day to day. Considerable time is spent representing the administration in committee meetings. If the meeting concerns policy involving trustees or major department heads, the Fellow may content himself or herself with what has been called the "fly on the wall" role. The Fellow has much student contact, often made at the president's behest. Budget season may call for the intern's hand at number crunching, or a campus crisis may bring back one of the long night watches of the sort that contributed to the aging of college executives during the late 1960s (terminating the offices of several and bringing on the death of at least one). The Fellow sometimes acts as ghost writer for his or her superior, and usually is asked to prepare a lengthy commentary at the end of the year.

The Fellows Program, again, is not conducted as on-track training for a particular presidency or any presidency as such; it is conducted as a year of exposure to administrative life. One of the increments sometimes overlooked is that being a Fellow's mentor causes an incumbent president to analyze his or her own functions. Such reflection has been found to be one of the principal justifications for the program.

Personal apprenticeship has always had a role in presidential preparation. Strong institutional leaders of the recent past—such as Charles E. Odegaard of the University of Washington, William P. Tolley of Syracuse, and Henry M. Wriston of Brown—gathered assistants and young deans about them who, after a few years, were drawn off into presidencies of their own. In academe, professional relationships are such that presidential acolytes seldom stay on to climb to the top of their own institution. In a business corporation, on the other hand, the company head (with the help of professional search consultants) selects the person who, company directors willing and after the proper time sequence, becomes the next chief executive officer. For a college president to pick, much less train, his or her own successor (allowing, for the moment, that the trustees would approve) is usually acknowledged as bad form, even though it has sometimes been done. Unless the process takes long enough for the newcomer to win his or her own spurs, once the king and kingmaker has departed, faculty barons, along with a dean or two, prepare to enter the lists.

We have taken the position that the chief criteria of presidential effectiveness concern keen sensitivity to the personal edge of the executive's interplay with faculty colleagues. Interplay with trustees, discussed later, has the same criteria. Knowledge about how to deal with human sensitivities does not come from courses or even independent reading, although the books listed in the bibliography at the end of the preceding chapter can help. Learning to lead a college becomes a conscious experience if one acknowledges that more learning results from errors than from successes. And the reward is not necessarily an extra hair shirt for Sunday. The most tangible reward of the president's willingness to learn from errors is that they occur less frequently as his term goes on. The college or university president who makes the same error twice is not likely to be tolerated; nor should the president himself tolerate repetition of errors.

More could be done to prepare persons for senior academic executive offices, including the office of president, provost, and academic vice president. General administrative preparation would allow for differing talents and would also release participants from the onus of being marked for the crown. The most direct approach is Temple University's thirty-year practice of appointing an academic vice president as heir-presumptive of the presidency. Although this approach merely pushes the crucial decision down one level, it creates the impression that the institution is protected against both arbitrary and automatic succession. It also leaves the number-two spot exposed to on-the-job training, but the procedure is a generally sound one since academic vice presidents nearly always come up the academic channels.

Still another form of training that is attractive to those who look forward to full-time academic life is the rotating presidency, which the British university vice chancellors have followed for decades. British vice chancellors hold a position comparable to that of the American college president for from two to five years, but retain their faculty union card and can return to their teaching positions before they run entirely out of friends among the faculty. By the same token, leading professors generally learn of their future move before they are tapped for the top administrative post; thus they can, to an extent, study the chart ahead for them. The rotating system is rarely used in the United States except on a temporary basis; it is also occasionally used in small communal institutions just getting under way or in institutions with chronic troubles. It is a fairly common device for the selection and changing of deans.

The system has its weaknesses: it does not allow for continuous growth of leadership, and it tacitly characterizes the presidency, though labeled differently, as a form of solitary penance. An inexorable result of the job's expansion into one of the most complex within a large organization is that most of the new British universities and some of the old ones now have permanent vice chancellors; in 1966 the Lord Franks commission recommended a permanent position for Oxford but settled for extending the term of office.

If learning presidential leadership is a conscious exercise in perception and self-control, it had best be linked with whatever other human tasks demand the same sorts of skills. In addition, however, college leadership has elements that give the experience a content and a flavor (to some, mildly bitter) all its own.

The Learning Context of Presidential Leadership

This chapter began with an analysis of what a potential president ought to know about college life and the educative process, matters that are less customarily taken up by search committees than might be supposed. In the following section we shall look for what is needed beyond a general knowledge of the job and the structure of higher education institutions; that is, what may be particularly true and important about the particular institution and what the new president will require in order to make good as an acknowledged leader of the institution.

The College's Past and Present Setting

It is a truism that few institutions move entirely away from their background. The circumstances leading to the institution's founding may have changed decades ago. Still, if the board of control remains self-perpetuating and retains the same affiliations—public, religious, or independent—the campus will reflect its origin in numerous ways, most prominently in its constituencies both on campus and among its clientele. Campus dress used to signal certain social differences, but the waning years of the 1960s, when the youth generation took over, saw the obliteration of most social distinctions. Some colleges have a strong regional flavor. Others—such as Princeton, Dartmouth, Mount Holyoke, and Hamilton—have unusually strong alumni influence. Still others reflect a denominational ambiance long after church control has ended. A church influence that persists more tangibly—and students' attitudes today have reinforced this influence on a number of campuses—may affect the value orientation if not the content of the course of study, as well as the composition of the student body. In the so-called committed Christian colleges, the influence may extend to constraints on conduct affecting both students and faculty. Although academic freedom is not necessarily abridged, a few institutions still require, for example, that evolution be taught "as one theory."

Other traditions may include relations with the surrounding community. For centuries, town and gown in Europe have drawn their dividing lines. They continue to do so, to varying degrees, in our country. The lines are particularly distinct when the institution is located in a small town but draws a cosmopolitan student body that contrasts with the surroundings, or when the institution, perhaps made possible by a large benefaction and then built as a single project in a region chosen arbitrarily, continues to be regarded as something of an alien presence. Conservative Portland, Oregon, for example, viewed Reed College guardedly for decades; in the late 1930s it was popularly viewed as "a center of communism, atheism, and free love." The college has been in existence for seventy years, but only in the past ten years, under the attentions of President Paul Bragdon and with the impetus of a major, long-range, philanthropic program from a local corporation executive, has Reed been generally welcomed as an indigenous member of the Portland community.

All such specific intelligence can hardly be absorbed by an entering president prior to accession. The main facts, to be sure, should be discussed with him or her prior to election. If the new executive is to grow into a leader, he or she will do well to study the setting, including its recent as well as its founding years, intensively and soon. The dynamics of college leaders and their followers are thus highly susceptible to the attitude of the faculty, students, and patrons toward their institution. Unfortunately, the president is often left to stumble along the path over obstacles that are the result of local circumstances, thus damaging what might otherwise become a successful leading performance. The only preventive is to learn early the full story of the community from a variety of sources chosen with care.

The record of a president's immediate predecessor is a fact of life for which no successor is responsible but that all too often casts strong influence on subsequent events. To an extent, the situation can become a Catch-22. If the former executive was highly regarded and perhaps held office for a long time, the successor will be regarded as a step down the scale until the nostalgia wears off. If the predecessor was a flop, expectations for broad-scale corrective action will be loud and immediate. If the previous administration was benevolently so-so, the members of the community will have turned their loyalties and demands to other sectors of the campus for service, thus requiring of the new president a major effort to gather in the reins of governance. Once again, learning about leadership becomes bound up in analysis and strategic planning appropriate to the problems at hand.

The Local Campus's Role in Institutional Leadership

Governance itself varies widely from college to college. The process of making decisions about education or campus policy reveals much about the character of leadership at the institution. In specialized professional schools such as engineering or agriculture, decision making about education policy will tend to reflect the objectivity of subject and, as well, a rather specified order of command. Liberal arts colleges and universities, on the other hand, usually experience the normal conflicts involved in choosing which learning is of greatest importance and to what extent the learner can help frame the teaching process. At this point, presidents from the more ordered disciplines sometimes show impatience with delays and controversies over what, whom, and how to teach. The effects can spill over into the regulation of campus life. In the tumultuous days of 1968–70, the colleges of applied science and arts were quietest; the activity was greatest at the centers of humanities and behavioral studies. (Some administrators were surprised when disruption mounted in the mathematics building at Columbia University.)

For a president to plan a strategy of governance, including the degree of faculty and student participation anticipated, is to take too narrow a view of human nature. Students of institutional organization—such as John Millett, Victor Baldridge, Frederick Balderston, and Morris Keeton—offer a range of predictions about the degree of democracy in campus governance in the future. Active faculty input into academic policy is and has been part of institutional governance, but there is general agreement that union contracts, if they continue, will restrict the faculty members' role as quasi-management officers. Faculty officers are appearing more frequently as contributing members at governing board committee meetings and also at full trustee meetings. Moreover, it is also agreed that the vast increase in age span and the relative maturity of undergraduate students today presage an enlarged role for them in governance systems throughout the college structure.

The degree of direct administration expected of the president varies from campus to campus, and adjusting to these expectations is yet another learning experience for the new executive. The president's own beliefs and style will, in turn, provide lessons for the campus to ponder. Unless the new chief executive is committed to making wholesale changes more or less unilaterally, the institution will generally tolerate a variety of styles of policy decision sharing, many of which existed on only a few campuses before 1970 (see Chapter 3). The president, to borrow once more from Burns's *Leadership*, may discover that the dispersion of institutional purpose through a functioning governing council is an effective way of enlisting wider leadership among the followers that make up a college community. For an outlook that is pertinent if perhaps oversimplified, a college executive might ponder the statement made by a young woman who had been chosen teacher of the year in St. Louis: "Developing human potential is not just important; it is all there is."[2]

Presidential Leadership and the Board of Trustees

The foregoing discussion may seem to imply that presidential leadership can be learned if the president has a keen set of sensory receptors, in particular an eye for the human realities within the institution. The reader may have the impression that leadership of peers cannot be taught in a classroom. One-on-one teaching, in some instances, may be effective; several strong presidents have trained their own assistants and backed them when college search committees came to the campus seeking a president for their own institution. However, our discussion of the presidential search procedure makes clear that the surest way to produce a significant leader begins at the source, that is, with the selection of a person who shows quality and experience in directing the education community and the learning process within.

2. *New York Times*, 17 February 1981, p. C4.

The time limits of the Presidency Project did not make possible the inclusion of trustees in the series of interviews held at the twenty-five institutions. Therefore, we must borrow from other studies, such as those made by the Association of Governing Boards of Universities and Colleges.

Trustees have been studied in numerous ways. Boards of trustees are usually weighted toward business corporations and the law. Philanthropists among them have, to be sure, made crucial differences in the status of many institutions, usually private. (The greatest amount of money yet donated is the $100 million given in 1980 to Emory University by Robert Woodruff of Coca-Cola.) In times of stress both inside and outside the campus, the academic community looks to the trustees as stabilizers. Their most important role, selecting a president, is then put to the test as the selected candidate asks for the board's backing. A few presidents have carried out long tenures, in spite of faculty and student protest, on the strength of the support of resolute if embattled trustees.

On the whole, however, the most effective board of trustees is one that supplements its financial and moral support with an ability to help the president carry out the mission of the college in ways that hold the college community together. There is an essential difference between constituency disagreements that occur in the process of making governance decisions and the organized anarchy proclaimed by Cohen and March. That difference can be supplied by an informed board whose collective judgment, especially that of its executive committee, becomes a base of reference for a new president.

Too often the president and the trustees fail to share their expertise when discussing institutional policy. The process is often best carried out in reports to the trustees—in particular, the annual report. By analyzing and then compiling the college or university's plans, hopes, and problems in such a way that intelligent lay persons can return their wisest consideration, the president not only enlightens the stewardship of the enterprise; simultaneously he or she comes to see that enterprise in broader perspective for having presented it systematically to the board.

Boards of trustees, like most boards of directors, are given to plenary meetings, where unruffled execution of the agenda is the chairperson's main concern, a sentiment that most board members trained in corporation meetings share. An elderly trustee, seasoned by years of governing sessions, once remarked after the full board meeting, "All you have to know on that board are three words—'I so move.'"

That advice does not apply to the board committees: academic affairs, students, buildings and grounds, development, and, to be sure, budget. The president, as an ex officio member of these committees, can ill afford to miss any of them. Moreover, he or she will urge the board chairperson to attend as many as possible. And success will be proportionate to the spirit in which constructive issues and arguments are raised.

Since the beginning of the 1970s, faculty and student representation on college committees has become common practice. Important contacts take place in such sessions. The presence of a professor or student at the plenary meeting, on the other hand, is reported in the press as an indication of spreading democracy; yet plenary sessions seldom make the news. The committee sessions, in contrast, can mix levels of the various constituencies so that the thoughts of professors, students, and board members are exchanged in the interest of the satisfactory resolution of an issue. In that spirit the Yale Corporation has for years required that every Fellow (trustee) spend a few days each year in residence at one of the undergraduate colleges.

In these ways the interchange between administration and trustees sets up a dialogue out of which can arise better understanding by both sides of what the university or college ought to accomplish. The trustees can thus prompt the chief executive to his or her best level of thinking about the leadership mission to be fulfilled. A good trustees meeting can offer an accurate review of what is going on inside the campus; an excellent trustees meeting goes beyond to lay out the guidelines for future accomplishment. To this extent, the president becomes the leader of an advanced class of institutional thinkers—men and women who can help build the bridge between academe and a surrounding world of immediate demands. At this top level is thus fulfilled an exhortation of William Boyd, former president of the University of Oregon, as he faced higher education's future:

> We've got to become teachers. There has been a profound igno-
> rance about the facts of economic and political life within the
> university communities because presidents have not adequately
> taught faculty, staff, and students what the situation is so that they
> understand it and are equipped to deal with and to help change it.
> Similarly, we have not [taught] external constituents—regents,
> legislators and the general public—about the great needs of
> higher education and its value to society. . . . There has been a
> default in leadership throughout our society; one of the ways in

which we see it manifested is in the failure of the teaching mission that is one of the most important responsibilities of a leader.[3]

Many administrators have had the great fortune to work not only with faculty who were ready to hear the facts but with a steady succession of trustees, men and women, who seldom missed the most important solutions in considering alternatives for action. Just who taught whom is not the significant point. As Boyd reminds us, in the free exchange of thought among people who care about their students and their enterprise lies the best opportunity for a president to learn to lead. If board members have been chosen for the wrong reasons, their resulting decisions will almost inevitably reveal these mistakes, and the college will shuffle along its way. If they are persons of a stature equal to the opportunity that the college daily faces—developing individual human potential to its fullest capabilities—then the institution will grow while the president's ability to lead grows as well. The best of presidents will regard the latter phenomenon as no more than accessory to the first.

The college president of the future will not be a different species from presidents of the present and past. Human limitations remaining what they are, society can perhaps look forward to a gradually improved understanding of how those limitations may be offset by greater knowledge of complex social organizations and how those organizations can be effectively led.

Many students of organizations believe that the perceptions of Chester I. Barnard, expressed in *The Functions of the Executive* (1938), will continue to hold true for institutions and executive behavior in the future. Though not primarily a philosopher, Barnard made some comments about individuals that apply as well to the future college executive as to any leader of a complex society. His points make an appropriate conclusion for this consideration of what college and university leadership may bring:

> An important characteristic of individuals is activity; and this in its . . . observed aspects is called behavior. Without it there is no individual person.

> The behavior of individuals we shall say [is] the result of psychological factors . . . the combination . . . of the physical, biological and social factors which have determined the history and the present state of the individual in relation to his present environment.

3. "Higher Education: Tough Times Ahead," *WICHE Reports*, Autumn 1980, p. 5.

We grant to persons the power of choice, the capacity of determination, the position of a free will. . . . This seems necessary to preserve a sense of personal integrity. . . . We observe that persons who have no sense of ego . . . , who have no initiative whatever, are problems . . . , unfitted for cooperation.

The attempt to limit the conditions of choice, so that it is practicable to exercise the capacity of will, is called making or arriving at a "purpose."

It is necessary to impress upon the reader the importance of this statement of the properties of persons. . . . No construction of the theory of cooperative systems or of organizations . . . can be made that is not based on some position as to the psychological forces of human behavior.[4]

Optimism for the future college president could lie in the fact that each generation produces tirelessly active persons who are capable of exercising their free will and appreciating their own ego and also of reckoning the limitations of human choice among one's peers and fellow workers. Chester Barnard's comments give further ground for optimism that a reasonable balance can be maintained—a balance between the will of the leader and the judgment of superior men and women who, through their leadership, will dedicate their energies to the continued improvement of higher learning in this country.

4. Chester I. Barnard, *The Functions of the Executive* (Cambridge, Mass.: Harvard University Press, 1938), pp. 13–14.

Bibliography

Andersen, Charles J., comp. *1980 Fact Book for Academic Administrators*. Washington, D.C.: American Council on Education, 1980.

Astin, Alexander W., and Scherrei, Rita A. *Managing Colleges for Maximum Effectiveness*. San Francisco: Jossey-Bass, 1979.

Baird, Leonard L.; Hartnett, Rodney T.; et al. *Understanding Student and Faculty Life*. San Francisco: Jossey-Bass, 1980.

Baldridge, J. Victor; Curtis, David V.; et al. *Policy Making and Effective Leadership: A National Study of Academic Management*. San Francisco: Jossey-Bass, 1978.

Barnard, Chester I. *The Functions of the Executive*. rpt. Cambridge, Mass.: Harvard University Press, 1968.

Bauer, Douglas. "Why Big Business Is Firing the Boss," *The New York Times Magazine*, 8 March 1981, pp. 22-25, 79-91.

Bennis, Warren G. *The Leaning Ivory Tower*. San Francisco: Jossey-Bass, 1973.

Bolman, Frederick deW. "Can We Prepare Better College and University Administrators?" *Undergraduate Education*, pp. 230-32. Current Issues in Higher Education. Washington, D.C.: Association for Higher Education, National Education Association, 1964.

———. *How College Presidents Are Chosen*. Washington, D.C.: American Council on Education, 1965.

Bowen, Howard R. *Investment in Learning: The Individual and Social Value of American Higher Education*. San Francisco: Jossey-Bass, 1977.

———. *The Costs of Higher Education*. San Francisco: Jossey-Bass, 1980.

Burke, Joseph C. "Coping with the Role of College or University President," *Educational Record*, Fall 1977, pp. 388-402.

Burns, James MacGregor. *Leadership*. New York: Harper and Row, 1978.

Capen, Samuel P. *The Management of Universities*. Buffalo: Foster and Steward, 1953.

Carnegie Council on Policy Studies in Higher Education. *Three Thousand Futures: The Next Twenty Years for Higher Education*. San Francisco: Jossey-Bass, 1980.

Cheit, Earl F. *The New Depression in Higher Education: A Study of Financial Conditions at Forty-one Colleges and Universities*. Carnegie Commission on the Future of Higher Education. New York: McGraw-Hill, 1971.

Chickering, Arthur W. *The Modern American College*. San Francisco: Jossey-Bass, 1981.

Cohen, Michael D., and March, James G. *Leadership and Ambiguity: The American College President*. New York: McGraw-Hill, 1974.

Cottle, Thomas J. *College: Reward and Betrayal*. Chicago: University of Chicago Press, 1977.

Cowley, W. H. *Presidents, Professors and Trustees: The Evolution of American Academic Government*. Edited by D. T. Williams, Jr. San Francisco: Jossey-Bass, 1980.

Dressel, Paul L. *Handbook of Academic Evaluation: Assessing Institutional Effectiveness, Student Progress, and Professional Performance for Decision Making in Higher Education*. San Francisco: Jossey-Bass, 1976.

Dodds, Harold W., et al. *The Academic President: Educator or Caretaker?* New York: McGraw-Hill, 1962.

Education Commission of the States. *Challenge, Coordination, and Governance in the 1980's*. Denver, Colo.: ECS, 1980.

El-Khawas, Elaine. *Special Policy Issues in Management of Student Aid*. Washington, D.C.: American Council on Education, 1980.

Etzioni, Amitai. *A Comparative Analysis of Complex Organizations*. rev. ed. New York: Free Press, 1975.

Feldman, Kenneth A., and Newcomb, Theodore M. *The Impact of College on Students*. San Francisco: Jossey-Bass, 1969.

Gaff, Jerry G. *Toward Faculty Renewal: Advances in Faculty, Instructional, and Organizational Development*. San Francisco: Jossey-Bass, 1976.

Hazen Foundation. *The Student in Higher Education.* Committee on the Student in Higher Education. New Haven, Conn.: 1968.

Hesburgh, Theodore M. "The College Presidency: Life between a Rock and a Hard Place," *Change,* May-June 1979, pp. 43–47.

Hesburgh, Theodore M.; Miller, Paul A.; and Wharton, Clifton R., Jr. *Patterns for Lifelong Learning.* San Francisco: Jossey-Bass, 1973.

Jencks, Christopher, and Riesman, David. *The Academic Revolution.* New York: Doubleday, 1968.

Katz, Joseph, et al. *No Time for Youth: Growth and Constraint in College Students.* San Francisco: Jossey-Bass, 1968.

Kauffman, Joseph F. *The Selection of College and University Presidents.* Washington, D.C.: Association of American Colleges, 1974.

———. "The New College President: Expectations and Realities," *Educational Record,* Spring 1977, pp. 146–68.

———. *At the Pleasure of the Board: The Service of the College and University President.* Washington, D.C.: American Council on Education, 1980.

Keezer, Dexter M. *The Light That Flickers: A View of College Education Which Contrasts Promise and Performance and Suggests Improvement.* New York: Harper, 1947.

Kemerer, Frank R., and Baldridge, Victor J. *Unions on Campus: A National Study of the Consequences of Faculty Bargaining.* San Francisco: Jossey-Bass, 1975.

Kerr, Clark. *The Uses of the University.* rev. ed. Cambridge, Mass.: Harvard University Press, 1972.

Maguire, John D. "The President as Educational Leader," *The President as Educational Leader.* Washington, D.C.: Association of American Colleges, 1976.

McGrath, Earl J. *The Graduate School and the Decline of Liberal Arts.* New York: Teachers College, Columbia University, 1959.

Meyer, H. E. "Headhunters Come Upon Golden Days," *Fortune,* 9 October 1978, pp. 100–102.

Millet, John D. *New Structures of Campus Power: Sucess and Failures of Emerging Forms of Institutional Governance.* San Francisco: Jossey-Bass, 1978.

Minter, John W., and Bowen, Howard R. *Independent Higher Education.* Washington, D.C.: National Association of Independent Colleges, 1978.

Mortimer, Kenneth P., and McConnell, T. R. *Sharing Authority Effectively: Participation, Interaction, and Discretion.* San Francisco: Jossey-Bass, 1978.

Nason, John W. *Presidential Search.* Washington, D.C.: Association of Governing Boards of Universities and Colleges, 1979.

————. *Presidential Assessment.* Washington, D.C.: Association of Governing Boards of Universities and Colleges, 1980.

National Center for Education Statistics. *Digest of Education Statistics.* Washington, D.C.: NCES, May 1980.

Parker, Gail T. *The Writing on the Wall: Inside Higher Education in America.* New York: Simon & Schuster, 1979.

Perry, William G. *Forms of Intellectual and Ethical Development in the College Years.* New York: Holt, Rinehart & Winston, 1970.

Raushenbush, Esther. *The Student and His Studies.* Middletown, Conn.: Wesleyan University Press, 1964.

Richman, Barry M., and Farmer, Richard N. *Leadership, Goals, and Power in Higher Education: A Contingency and Open Systems Approach to Effective Management.* San Francisco: Jossey-Bass, 1974.

Riley, Gary L., and Baldridge, J. Victor, eds. *Governing Academic Organizations: New Problems, New Perspectives.* Berkeley: McCutchan, 1977.

Rourke, Francis E., and Brooks, Glenn E. *The Managerial Revolution in Higher Education.* Baltimore: The Johns Hopkins University Press, 1966.

Rudolph, Frederick. *Curriculum: A History of the American Undergraduate Course of Study Since 1636.* San Francisco: Jossey-Bass, 1977.

Sanford, Nevitt. *The American College.* New York: Wiley, 1962.

Selden, William. "How Long Is a College President?" *AAC Bulletin.* Washington, D.C.: Association of American Colleges, 1960.

Sloan Commission on Government and Higher Education. *A Program for Renewed Partnership.* Cambridge, Mass.: Ballinger, 1980.

Smith, Virginia B., and Bernstein, Alison R. *The Impersonal Campus: Options for Reorganizing Colleges to Increase Student Involve-*

ment, Learning, and Development. San Francisco: Jossey-Bass, 1979.

Stoke, Harold W. *The American College President*. New York: Harper & Brothers, 1959.

Walberg, Herbert J. "The Academic President: Colleague, Administrator, or Spokesman?" *Educational Record*, Spring 1969, pp. 194–99.

Walker, Donald E. *The Effective Administrator: A Practical Approach to Problem Solving, Decision Making, and Campus Leadership*. San Francisco: Jossey-Bass, 1979.

White, Robert W. *Lives in Progress*. 3rd ed. New York: Holt, Rinehart & Winston, 1975.

Western Interstate Commission for Higher Education. "Higher Education: Tough Times Ahead," *WICHE Reports*, Autumn 1980, pp. 5–7.